BECOMING THE ENTITY DOCTOR

A Guide to Discovering The Spiritual World

Cindy Hallett

BecomingTheEntityDoctor.com

Becoming The Entity Doctor

A Guide to Discovering

The Spiritual World

Cindy Hallett

Copyright © 2023 Stand in the Light, LLC

ISBN: 979-8-9885211-0-5

First Printing October 2023

Cindy Hallett

Stand in the Light, LLC

5108 Cree Lane

Austin, TX 78734

833-612-4100

www.ComeStandInTheLight.com

www. BecomingTheEntityDoctor.com

Cindy Hallett is available to speak at your business or conference event on a variety of topics. Call 833-612-4100 for booking information.

The Easiest and Most Breathtaking Way to Change Your Life

Discover how becoming aware of the energy around you can make it easier to manifest your desires. Learning to raise your vibration is the simplest way to make lasting changes in your life.

This book will start you on your path and help you recognize the good and evil you may encounter along the way. Acquiring simple, energetic techniques can help you live a happier, stress-free life and step into a new, exciting chapter.

Follow Cindy, The Entity Doctor™, as she learns to work with energy, discovers unseen positive and negative energetic beings, and figures out how to resolve spiritual issues. Read all about her amazing experiences starting out in the metaphysical field, mastering techniques and processes directly from Spirit.

Learn about the different entities she encounters every day and the entities that may be around you.

As a professional, Cindy is constantly discovering new threats and determining how to resolve them. See how shifting your energy can improve your quality of life and allow you to find happiness. Want to learn more about influencing your future? Peek inside.

About the Author

Cindy Hallett is The Entity Doctor, a leading authority on unseen entities and energies. Working with Spirit and her guides and angels, Cindy has figured out how to remove unwanted and uninvited beings and the energy left behind from her clients' lives.

As a healer, The Entity Doctor sends energy through Reiki, ThetaHealing™, readings, and divinely led coaching and guidance.

Cindy resides in the beautiful hill country of central Texas with her husband and four-footed furry family. A former ballerina, she enjoys staying in shape and, of course, dancing, as well as cooking. An avid animal lover and communicator, she enjoys a full house filled with love and laughter.

Her business, Stand in the Light, LLC, started as an online crystal shop. Cindy loves selecting the finest rocks available and using her unique skills to seek out each crystal. Then she clears the energy from each crystal to make it work at its best for you.

TABLE OF CONTENTS

CHAPTER 1
WHERE IT BEGINS

In the quiet space between what we know and what we feel, I discovered an unseen world....

"You are good at working with the dark entities," this woman told me.

"Dark entities? I want to be a medium," I said. I had never even considered working with dark entities; that sounded scary. "Isn't that like being the garbage collector of the metaphysical world?" I asked.

The lady shrugged. "It's what you're good at," she replied.

Little did I know I had just met my best friend Lorna for the next several years.

I'm Cindy, and this is my story about being a public procurement manager and protector of the taxpayer dollar to becoming the entity doctor—a protector against dark entities—and an energy worker, healer, and teacher. You will share all my trials and tribulations, experiences, and pitfalls of this transformation as well as the exciting and sometimes frightening things I have learned along the way. Apparently, I agreed to awaken spiritually in my soul contract before I entered this life. One thing is for sure: if you have agreed to do something in your soul contract, you will be drawn there, maybe kicking and screaming, but your angels will get you where you need to go. What you do with it once you get there is up to you. The smartest thing is to listen and follow what Spirit is telling you. You may be very surprised at where you end up, and it may be better than you ever imagined.

I'm certainly not doing anything I had previously conceived of, but as Lorna said, I'm good at it, and it gives me joy. It was not an easy path to get here, and I will tell you about my personal experiences. Should you decide to embark on a journey into the world of spirituality, your experiences will be different from mine. My hope is that this book will give you some information to base your decision on, including whether spirituality is your path and a little about what you might expect along the way. The things Spirit has taught me are based on my energy signature and strengths; again, your lessons will be different, but all these lessons are magnificent.

As humans, we consist of four parts: physical, mental, emotional, and spiritual. We are taught all about the first three and little or nothing about developing our spiritual side. This includes our faith, intuition, and the ability to trust ourselves and others. This book will explore many aspects of learning about your spiritual side and some things I was unprepared for as my vibration rose. Learning to recognize and manipulate energy is very challenging. There are many ways to utilize this talent and ways it can turn on you.

Here are some things to ask yourself to see whether you are ready for this journey:

- Are you interested in developing or furthering your spiritual knowledge and talents?
- We all have spiritual gifts; do you recognize yours?
- Are you ready to enter the unseen world and work with your angels, guides, and highest self?
- Are you ready to find answers to some of your most tormented questions?
- Are you ready to adapt to the answers?

In this book, I will take you along as I learn how to figure out fundamental techniques all the way to an advanced understanding of negative energy and entity removal. And I'm still learning. You will share in my trials and errors, my growth and stagnation, and what I discovered along the way. Let me show you the pitfalls I encountered so you can try to avoid them for yourself, or at least be ready and know you will get through them.

You never know where life will take you, and it's not usually where you are expecting or even wanting to go.

"I want to be a ballerina!" said the little girl who grew up to be an accountant.

"I want to be a fireman!" said the little boy, now a contractor. We all find our niche, our gifts, and the area where we excel.

Like doctors each have their own specialty, so do metaphysicians. Patch.com has defined a metaphysician as:

"A metaphysical doctor uses holistic healing. They know a variety of tools to help heal at the spirit level. Seeing a metaphysical doctor in addition to your medical doctor can be very useful when you want wellness for your whole being focusing in on body, mind and spirit."

Mar 3, 2012

When I began studying spirituality, I wasn't aware of all the possibilities, and I wasn't even aware that an entity doctor even existed. We usually hear about mediums and psychics. Here are a few more spiritual modalities you might be familiar with; you might even be drawn to one of these areas.

Information Practitioners:	Energy Workers:
➢ Readers	➢ Massage Therapists
➢ Astrologers	➢ Acupuncturists
➢ Palmists	➢ Pranic Healers
➢ Numerologists	➢ Reiki Practitioners
➢ Psychometrists	➢ Feng Shui Practitioners
➢ Shamans	➢ ThetaHealers™

You might be asking, "What is an entity doctor?"

As an entity doctor, I am able to detect external entities that are attached to people, places, and things. I can tell you what type of entities these are, how many of them there are of each kind, and if any are extremely powerful or dangerous. I can detect and repair damage to the soul from any lifetime, remove spells, seal portals, and address various other issues that we will discuss later. In addition, I practice many forms of energy healing, such as Reiki and ThetaHealing™.

For this book, we will focus on developing the entity removal gifts.

An entity doctor is your first stop as you embark down the road of spirituality. To be able to make progress in addressing your inner self, it is best to have any parasites and clutter removed in advance. For example, imagine you are ready to plant new seeds in your garden, but last year's growth has overtaken the bed. The entity doctor will remove the thorny vines, leaves, and overgrowth to get down to the fresh fertile soil so you can easily grow unencumbered by external forces.

It is not easy to find sources to learn about these dark issues. I was lucky to learn the basics of entity removal from my first spiritual teacher, and from there, I listened to guidance from Spirit. Spirit has many names. You select the energy that you find best: God, Source Creator, the Universe, Jesus, Muhammed, Buddha, Allah; it's your choice.

I will tell you what I have learned from Spirit; some things you will resonate with, and other things will not suit you. Everyone is different, and the information you learn will go into one of three categories;

1. I accept this theory and put it into practice.
2. I reject this theory.
3. Someone believes this, so it may be a workable theory. I'll keep an eye on it.

"I just finished building this house; it was such a nightmare. We have moved in, and everything is going wrong. Can you help me?"

I could hear the desperation and helplessness in Brittany's voice. I said, "Let's check in and see what's going on."

I asked Brittany about her family, home, and pets. I connected with my Spirit council and asked several questions about each family member, home, and property. I spoke with each of the animals who were willing to talk and discovered the problem.

"You have two underworld portals coming into your home; the dog told me where they are."

Brittany protested. "That's impossible! This is a brand new house."

I asked, "Okay, how long has the land been there? What has happened on this property in the past?"

Brittany agreed that we couldn't account for the history of the land.

I closed and sealed the portals and cleared the home, property, and family members that needed clearing. I cleansed and healed each one and cut their cords. Brittany reported back that the energy in the house was totally different. The fights and frights had stopped, and everyone was calmly enjoying their new home. Even the animals were getting along.

Brittany checked back with me every three months at first to see if any tune-up sessions were needed to maintain her freedom from negative attachments. Now she checks back when the energy in her home or of any of her family members feels off. So she knows I'm here for her whenever she needs me.

Are you ready to begin or accelerate your spiritual experience? You can be anything where your talents excel; you don't have to be an entity doctor. You can explore the possibilities, and as your gifts develop, Spirit will guide you toward your best fit. When you are ready, teachers will present themselves, and you can take your studies as far as you like. You may use your new skills as your profession, or you can play and have fun with your gifts for yourself. Knowing how to ask Spirit questions and confidently receive the answers will help you and your family in the future.

The first step is learning to raise your vibration. This opens you to communicate with Spirit and find your happiest path toward your goal, which may be better than you ever imagined. Take the first step with me.

CHAPTER 2
IN YOUR WAY

"I've been looking for help for so long," Kathy told me. "I'm always depressed and tired. I've been to my doctor and had all the tests, but they can't find anything. I don't want to go on mood-altering drugs; I want to get back to being me."

I tuned into Kathy and found that she had a significant number of lost souls attached and an underworld portal which means unlimited underworlds on her. She was ridden with negative stimuli, which is why she felt so bad. She couldn't "will herself" into feeling better because the problem was external and not something Kathy could control. I explained what was wrong and how much it would cost to fix it. I told her it would only take an afternoon and a few days of recovery. Kathy said she would think about it.

The next time I heard from Kathy was a text a few months later complaining about how bad she felt and that she couldn't take it anymore, but she never scheduled her clearing; she wouldn't commit the time, finances, and attention to clear up the issue. I would sympathize and say, "I'm sure with that many entities, you feel terrible. When do you want to schedule your clearing?" These texts continued for over a year. Kathy never did get cleared. She eventually stopped contacting me regularly, but I hear from her occasionally.

Are you serious about learning to communicate with Spirit, raising your vibration, and finding your joy? In that case, you must commit to focusing on incorporating this into your everyday life. When you learn to dance, play an instrument, play a sport, learn a language, or anything else, you must practice. I love the old joke;

A tourist goes to New York City, climbs into a cab, and asks the driver:

"How do you get to Carnegie Hall?"

The driver responds, "Practice, practice, practice."

Many people who contact me for help explain that they don't have the time to commit to becoming spiritual; they just want it to happen. Many people believe that spirituality is magic, and I agree. However, it takes time and requires consistent effort. Like anything worth your attention, if you don't *have* the time for it, you *find* or *make* the time. The good news is that the practice of raising your vibration is much more laid-back than the other activities mentioned above.

With this in mind, this book will not teach you to become an entity doctor and battle dark entities any more than reading a book on becoming a ski jumper prepares you to strap on your first pair of skis and head for the launch. Your goal may be the PhD but you must start with 101.

I talk to people who tell me they have no psychic abilities; they are in awe of people who do. They say that they don't receive messages or know what is going to happen before it does. They are totally without any intuition whatsoever. One of my first classes was animal communication. We were taken to a stable and told to ask the horse how old she was. About 65 percent of the students said the horse told them she was 16; the teacher verified this. I didn't hear anything.

In another class, they brought in a dog, and we asked him questions; my answers were different from the majority of the students. Was I making up my answers? Was I connected to another dog, or did I want to hear these animals so badly that my subconscious took control and tried to give me what I wanted? How do you tell the difference? How do you know when it's you and when it's real? How do you get out of your own way?

When we talk about getting out of your own way, this means looking beyond all the preconceived notions and beliefs from this lifetime and past lives that work against you. Sometimes it's your tendencies that make trouble; other times, it's the part of your zodiac sign that drives you nuts about yourself. You're probably making a list of these now. Let me tell tales about myself. I am a petite, redheaded, left-handed, A-personality Virgo. What does this mean?

Petite means short; we wee ones live at a lower elevation than the average person. It is interesting because when I meet people, I receive energy from their torsos more than their heads. For me, the vertical challenge results in *small dog syndrome*. I must be noticed, included, and valued. If I am disrespected or disregarded, I growl and bite ankles like any small dog would. I don't really bite physically, but my energy and words can be biting. I'm sure you know a powerful petite bundle of dynamite. As William Shakespeare said,

"Though she be but little, she is fierce."

Redheaded people tend to be quick to anger, very stubborn, and tenacious. Not many people are willing to take me on in a controversial discussion. When I took a negotiations class as a procurement manager, the senior member of the class said he didn't want to partner with me for the negotiation assignment; I was too much for him. This makes me good at dealing with vendors and negative entities. I stick with my project until it is done, no matter what it takes.

Left-handed means I'm in my right mind. Right-handed people use their left brain more, making them logical, analytical, and methodical. Lefties tend to be more creative and have a unique perspective. We address problems from a different angle than most people. I can't tell you how many times someone has responded to my suggestion with:

"I would never have thought of that!"

I suppose this helps me get out of 3D thinking and get creative with solutions to removing various types of entities.

A-personality means I'm the boss! I'm in charge. As a procurement officer, I used my energy field to control a situation well. A-personalities are competitive and have a strong sense of urgency. We are impatient and can be hostile when we aren't achieving our goals. With these high standards, we stress out when we push ourselves too hard. In my procurement life, I was an overachiever. I worked sixty hours a week and sat on two prestigious boards of directors.

If I haven't painted enough of a high-strung picture, we get to Virgo. If you know any Virgos, you know them to be meticulous and anal-retentive. This person handles the organization and details of whatever comes up. When I close a portal, I don't close it once; I put on four layers and then cure the seal to ensure it stays entirely inaccessible to the bad guys. This nit-pickiness is how I drive myself crazy. The strive for perfectionism takes much longer than less stringent people might take to do a job, but I haven't had a portal reopen yet, so it's worth it.

With all these personality traits put together, you can see why Spirit selected me to be The Entity Doctor: I take no flak from entities, and what I start, I finish. On the other hand, if becoming a spiritual being means relaxing, releasing control, and allowing, you can see how that has been a struggle for me. It shows you that if I can do it, you can too. Some clients want me to be the patient and compassionate coach where they can cry on my shoulder, and I will stroke their hair and tell them, "It's not your fault."

Instead, I tell them, "If you aren't ready to take responsibility for your own happiness, I'm not the right person to help you."

They don't really want help anyway. I am patient and compassionate with people who want to develop their spiritual side and are willing to put in the practice.

When I talk with a new client, many times the conversation begins with them saying,

"You're going to think I'm crazy, but…"

"You're not going to believe this, but…"

People, especially those with the ability to see, hear, or feel, will be hesitant about revealing these gifts. They are afraid of being ridiculed and called crazy. I've got news for you: everyone is crazy in their own way. Yes, you too, and me.

Think of each family member; you can identify the area of crazy for all of them.

The fear of revealing your gifts may stem from childhood when a friend or parent ridiculed or mocked you for talking about your experiences. Some people turn off their gifts, choosing not to listen to the messages that Spirit is sending them. Other people retain the gift but suffer in silence, not knowing who to trust with what can sometimes be harrowing experiences. They might receive a message and ask, "Is this scary? Is this from a friend or something trying to trick me? Can I trust this information? What do I do with this information?"

Without a point of reference or a sounding board, this situation is overwhelming and confusing, with nowhere to turn. So you get frightened and depressed and are afraid to reveal yourself to your friends and family. Where do you go to learn about the information you are receiving?

Another issue people get tangled up with is what their religious leaders have taught them and how it fits with becoming unique spiritual individuals. One of the ladies in my advanced class, Natalie, is a talented biomagnetism therapist and Reiki energy practitioner. She does healings using magnets placed strategically on the client incorporating Reiki energy. She has worked on me and does a fabulous job.

Natalie was raised Catholic and felt a conflict between being unfaithful to God and learning to listen directly to Spirit. This conflict hinders her from getting out of her own way and believing the information she receives. When we were reading clients in class, she would always talk last and sound a little unsure of herself, although her information always rang true.

She says she doesn't see or feel, but on one occasion, I was on her massage table, and she was doing a treatment for me. I felt an angel working on my legs to the right of me. Natalie got up from the stool at my feet, walked around the angel, and came up to my head. She could have walked straight up the side of the table and through the angel if she didn't feel its presence, but she walked around it. I'm sure this wasn't a conscious act, and she was surprised when I told her about it, but she obviously felt it there.

Some religions teach that only the officiant—priest, minister, rabbi, or cardinal—can connect with God or that this can only be done in a place of worship. Any deviation from this is a sin worthy of an eternity in hell. If this is ingrained at an early age, I can see how someone seeking Spirit can stand in their own way.

We all have a little spark of God within us called our Highest Self. Learning to communicate with this inner spark, along with your guides and angels assigned to help you throughout your life, is the start of your journey, and isn't it nice to know that you have this divine team on your side? You are not alone on your journey, and they will help guide you along your path.

CHAPTER 3
MY JOURNEY

You may be looking at your list of personality traits that drive you crazy about yourself. Let's see if we can turn up your vibration to spin things around and see them as assets. My list of things still drives me up the wall, but I have learned to accept the benefits of having these strong qualities. This book will show you the unique spiritual gifts that you possess, teach you to enter the unseen world and work with your angels, guides, and highest self, and work together to find the answers you seek.

You will learn to work with energy to manifest what is in your best and highest good. As I found out, it can be a surprise. Spirit will bring you the sweetest surprises; all you need to do is exude the energy you would like back. The following chapters will teach you to tune your energy to make life easier and show you through my experience what can happen if you decide to take your vibration higher and higher.

Thank you for joining me on my journey from a not-very-nice person-but-good-at-my-job to a much calmer and in touch spiritual individual to the energy worker on multiple levels as

The Entity Doctor. This ride has many bumps and a fair share of twists and turns. When I think I have something figured out, it turns out I was only half right; now, I must figure out the rest. Spirit keeps me challenged and definitely not bored.

We will talk about:

- How I got started.
- What is vibration?
- How do you know if you're psychic?
- The difference between entities and energies.
- How do you figure this stuff out?
- How Spirit helps out.
- How does it feel to work with energy?
- How dark does it go?
- Now we're getting weird!
- What else is there?
- Things aren't as they seem.

How I Got Started

It's extraordinary how Spirit will get you where you need to go, and even stranger that you go without questioning why; you just do it. Spirit took a long and winding path involving two continents and past life lovers to get me where I was supposed to be. I was eager to accept the next challenge once again without prior planning or forethought. That is not very Virgo of me.

I ended up in a spirituality class—nothing I had ever considered studying. When I was a teen, I had a bad experience with church and never returned. Religion and spirituality were nowhere near my radar, yet here I was. In Chapter 4, you will see how this class got me started learning the skills and knowledge I would need to make my occupation as an entity doctor. They introduced me to some of my best friends and colleagues and laid the groundwork for me to learn and grow in my field.

What Is Vibration?

Vibration is the frequency at which your energy as a living being vibrates. We all know low-vibrational people; they are low-energy and slow. As our vibration rises, we don't move faster; we are better able to connect with Spirit and our spiritual team. We are able to gain guidance and input from these unseen helpers. It sounds simple enough: "Raising your vibration."

Is it really that easy? Actually, no. Many things change. Join my client Mary in Chapter 5 as she experiences a drastic rise in her vibration in a short period of time and the information she receives. Spirit determines when you are ready for an upgrade in your vibration; they say how much and what you need to release as this happens. We are not usually prepared for this boost, yet here it comes. It's surprising what we find coming out the other side.

How Do You Know If You're Psychic?

Everyone is psychic. We all have a little voice that tells us what we should and shouldn't do. The problem is when this little voice doesn't align with our logical minds. Who is this little voice, and where does it come from? Who is right—the little voice or the logic? We will closely examine this and determine our best course of action in Chapter 6.

Since we know you are psychic, how do you receive information? There are six ways to receive information. Let's talk about them all and see your strongest gift. This will help you discern what information is most important and most relevant to you.

The Difference between Entities and Energies

"Entities and energies: I thought they were the same thing. I didn't know there was a difference." This is usually what I hear when checking someone for the first time. Energy is all around us; it comes in the form of light, sound, heat, and other stimuli. We are very good at interpreting energy; we have done so all our lives, and it is second nature. Chapter 7 delves into negative energy that makes you uncomfortable; this can be cleansed.

Entities are sentient beings. They may be in the physical or not. They may be here for our best and highest good or not. Dealing with entities is vastly different from energy. Although both must be addressed during a spirit clearing, I had to learn the order and procedures to remove each effectively.

How Do You Figure This Stuff Out?

Figuring out how to clear entities, what kind of entities we are dealing with, and the distinction between them can be a steep learning curve. I was lucky to find a good teacher, and I learned to listen to Spirit for the rest. In Chapter 8, we will discuss the two main types of entity attachments I find on people and how they differ.

Come with me to my very first clearing, and together we will see how to figure out what to do and when. It takes a lot of trial and error to see what works and elation and exhaustion when we succeed. I get attacked a lot, especially in the early days. I have survived, so it must be lessons that Spirit sends me to share the experience and to see how I am doing. If this is an issue you experience, you, too, can work through it with help.

How Spirit Helps Out

The energy you put out is the energy you get back. This is a universal law. So how do you adjust the energy you are putting out to create a better life for yourself? How do you tailor your energy to increase your vibration and achieve your desired results? Chapter 9 will explain this so you can become more aware of what you are calling into your reality.

As your vibration rises, you get more attention from both the light and the dark sides. There can be consequences that you should be aware of. As your vibration rises, you are able to take on more responsibility, and your spiritual team is thrilled!

How Does It Feel to Work with Energy?

Different types of energies feel very different. Clearing evil entities can be uncomfortable, distasteful, and sometimes painful. Doing healings can be quite comforting, warm, and loving. Occasionally, what you feel as you work on a client is not your own. We will determine how to tell the difference.

How do you send your consciousness into another dimension, and what does this look like? Chapter 10 will help you find out what it feels like to channel Spirit and the best way to deliver the messages that you receive. I get feelings about people I haven't met yet or clearings that are happening soon. You will discover what I feel during a clearing and how I tell whether my efforts succeeded.

How Dark Does It Go?

So I've learned about negative entities; what more could there be? HOLY COW! Hold on to your socks. Although not my first underworld portal, the story in Chapter 11 was my first huge one. This job taught me what is expected of an entity doctor and just how hard a good one must work to get the job done.

Moving up the dark ladder, we meet the bosses of the negative entities; Spirit calls them Karalians. Come along as I am introduced to this demonic entity. I must figure out the best approach to removing it and the energy it leaves behind. If I've given you the impression this stuff is easy, it's not.

Now We're Getting Weird!

I know you thought we got weird before, but more types of entities were revealed to me. These are different because some are physical, but not in this dimension. This makes the client very uncomfortable, but it is a challenge to track down the source. We have heard of aliens; well, there are numerous types with all different ulterior motives.

In Chapter 12, you will learn about the species that surprised me most: the Inner Earth beings. I had never heard of them; nobody taught me how to help them, and I was at a loss. Come with me as I figure out how to return these very aggressive creatures to their home.

What Else Is There?

Not all spiritual issues involve external entities. Many types of damage happen to the soul; it doesn't totally heal. When this happens, the emotion left in the scar can affect subsequent lifetimes until it is repaired. Soul damage results in many fears and phobias. See how damage from many lifetimes ago is affecting people today in Chapter 13.

Things Aren't as They Seem

For years, clients would come to me complaining of a powerful entity that nobody could remove. I was confident that I was the chosen one, and I would work like crazy to get rid of this malicious attachment. I would do my best work, go above and beyond the call, and it wouldn't have any effect on it. I called in my colleagues to discuss this situation and got many workable theories of what it might be. I finally think I have it figured out. Chapter 14 will show you that this is fascinating, although very difficult to fix.

I hope my story will inspire you to embark on your unique spiritual journey. You are not alone; you have your guides and angels making up your spiritual team. You can always find a mentor or fellow student to assist and accompany you on this journey into the unseen realm. Enjoy these experiences; they are as unique as you are.

Chapter 4
Learning About Spirituality

"Learning about spirituality? That sounds like fun."

I bet you have said that too. I was sitting at a psychic's table at a spiritual expo. I had never been to a spiritual expo; I'm unsure what drew me to this one. I was talking to a reader because I wanted an answer to a recent happening; my mom and I had recently returned from a river cruise in France. We traveled extensively after my dad transitioned and we always had a wonderful time together. I had met the captain of the riverboat, who spoke very little English. I speak no French, but somehow we connected energetically. He invited my mom and me to join him at his table for the captain's dinner. He danced only with me the entire night, and I felt so drawn to him.

I told the psychic, "I don't know what's going on; I'm not interested in a bilingual, intercontinental relationship with a man I've only met once. I'm happily married! Why can't I disconnect from this guy?"

She said, "You were lovers in a former life; you were killed, which left him with abandonment issues. You agreed between lives that when you were middle-aged, he would come and wake you up. Oh, and by the way, I do classes."

"Learning about Spirituality? That sounds like fun." I said, and my angels jumped for joy! This psychic turned into my first teacher, Topaz.

I had already begun studying energy work and achieved the level of Reiki master. I originally wanted to be an animal communicator and had taken a weekend workshop with Amelia Kinkade. She was attuned to picking up on how talented people are through their vibration. Several people in the class were recognized, but I wasn't.

In Topaz's class, there were twelve of us. The two ladies were extraordinary at the information they received and how they were able to channel it. Channeling means receiving information from Spirit and relaying this information to the intended recipient. It is interpreting or translating for Spirit.

Topaz would channel for us at the end of class. Once, she read several pages she had channeled from Jesus earlier that afternoon. I was in awe. How does this work? What would the ability to channel be like? Topaz regularly worked with a group of Spirits, calling themselves Cimmaron. She explained that her familiarity with the group of Spirits helped her connect and hear them well.

In one class, I was attempting to do a reading for Miranda, one of the extraordinary ladies, and I said, "I see a shadow; I think it's a square; no, maybe it's a triangle; no, it's a square." I wasn't getting any information at all.

Miranda looked at me and said, "Sandra is telling me that she misses you. Do you know a Sandra?"

"Not in this lifetime," I answered.

Topaz explained that Sandra was most likely someone from my soul group who wasn't cast in a role in this lifetime. I actually felt bad that I couldn't remember who Sandra was, but we aren't supposed to know those things while on this side of the veil.

Topaz taught us about developing a regular meditation practice, chakras, auras, signs and symbols, angels, guides, and all the basic ABCs of how this spirituality stuff works. I thoroughly enjoyed the class and getting to know my wonderful classmates. Topaz started an intermediate class, and more people joined. Several of them were advanced psychics and received unique and amazing information that they shared with the group. Still in awe, I felt jealous that they were receiving messages and I wasn't.

Topaz would bring a person into class for all of us to read, and then we would go around the room to share the information we received. One of the first people was her mom. I tuned in and, in my mind's eye, saw the silhouette of a cat sitting in front of a garden of flowers. When it came to my turn, I asked, "Do you have a cat?"

Topaz's mom burst into tears. Tears confirm that you have made a valid connection, but it is a bit alarming the first time.

Topaz said, "Her cat Emily has recently disappeared."

Her mom chimed in, "No, she said goodbye."

I began telling her what I had seen, and the information started to flow for me. "She went into a greenbelt and found a nice comfortable spot where she curled up and just let go. There was no violence, no pain, no fear; she just left her body, and that was it." This gave Topaz's mom comfort and closure.

A few days later, I was with Topaz for a private session, and she said, "I still don't understand the silhouette in the garden."

I said, "I figured that out; that's where Emily is now."

Topaz said she got chills. Chills or goosebumps are confirmation from Spirit that the information you are relaying or receiving is correct. Psychics rely upon this type of feeling to verify their readings, so note that when you feel a confirmation feeling, you will know you are right. This was the first time I would get out of my own way and believe the information flowing to me, and it was sent by a cat.

When I began studying spirituality, I didn't receive information that I could translate into meaning. As I worked with it, I began to be able to translate the information into meaning, as in the story of Emily. The more I worked on communicating with my guides and angels, the more familiar their energy became. I knew that I was connected to my spiritual team. As I started doing spirit clearings, I worked with my highest self for information about entity attachments when checking a client. I also worked with Archangel Michael for assistance in removing the dark entities.

The more I worked, the higher my vibration rose and the more information I received. You will hear stories of when Spirit was ready to give me an upgrade in vibration and how I was affected. Today I can connect with all the archangels and the Creator of All That Is and receive messages from deceased loved ones, animals, and councils consisting of angels, ascended masters, galactics, and many other souls. There are several councils that I connect with, depending on the situation and expertise of the council.

The only way to build your confidence as a psychic is to receive confirmation that your intuition is correct either from your client that they understand the message or by circumstances happening that you predicted. One of the hardest things, especially when starting out, is receiving information you don't understand. We try to make sense of this information. This is a mistake; messages should be delivered as they are received, whether the channeler understands them or not, and we usually don't.

Classes on spirituality are excellent investments if you are interested in learning different perspectives about how this stuff works. Use what you learn for yourself, your family, and friends, or you may decide to make your living doing spiritual work. Workshops and classes give you the opportunity to meet like-minded people, gain very valuable insights, explore different modalities, and make some of your best friends.

If you can find someone who is developing their skills alongside you, it's a great partnership. Lorna would tell me about things she discovered and her theories about how it all fits together, and I would be amazed. I would tell her about things I had recently figured out and how I thought things worked, and she would be fascinated. We would put our heads together to address whatever didn't make sense and would usually come up with workable theories.

Lorna had a network of intuitive friends and was good at keeping in touch with each of them. I would tell her, "I couldn't sleep at all last night; I woke up at three and never got back to sleep."

She would say, "Michele, Suzanne, and Kaya said the same thing; they woke up at three and never got back to sleep."

It was comforting to know that there was something bigger than any of us waking us up at precisely the same time. We didn't know what or why, but we all felt the same thing.

In another class, I met Mitchy. We were paired up to practice doing readings, and I read her little dog, who had recently passed away. This gave Mitchy peace and calm. Later in the class, we had an exercise to find the deceased loved one who was with us. This proved to be difficult for everyone in the class because the building where we were meeting used to be a biker hangout, and apparently, most of the deceased bikers returned to this building instead of going to the light. We were coming up with the most unusual names. I came up with Lucille; we couldn't figure out who this belonged to. At the break, Mitchy came up to me and said, "Lucille is for you." I was very surprised as I didn't know of any Lucilles in my family.

Later, Lorna did a reading for me and spoke with Lucille. My father's mother, my grandmother, was orphaned at the age of two or three in Chicago during one of the big fires. Lucille was her mother who perished during this fire. She had married a man who was a bit older than her that she believed would be successful in business and in love, and she was thrilled by the excitement of moving to the big city. After giving birth to my grandmother, Lucille realized that her husband wasn't the successful businessman she had dreamed of; life was dull and hard, and she was bored. The fire allowed her to restart her game and get on to the next incarnation. Lorna said Lucille is with me a lot of the time. I would have never known Lucille were it not for Mitchy; she has become a good friend and colleague. To this day, we call each other to get insight when we are stuck on a client or need a fresh perspective.

I've realized that we each have unique perspectives and receive different information from Spirit. Imagine we are all sitting in a giant warehouse without lights. We each hold a flashlight and can only see what our beam illuminates. You can't see into my beam, and I can't see into yours. This is why it takes a village to get well-rounded psychics.

Lorna taught me many things that she observed and was taught by Spirit, and I taught her the information I received. Together we helped each other unravel mysteries that we couldn't solve individually.

Like medical doctors, psychics are tasked with figuring out mysteries. Unlike medical doctors, we have unlimited and many times unknown elements to piece into the puzzle. We always learn new things, expanding our knowledge base and skill levels. One of the most fun parts of this job is that you are always learning and growing. Spirit and your friends will teach you how to handle spiritual situations as they arise. You will be stepping into your power. You will be powerful.

CHAPTER 5
YOUR VIBRATION

You've heard it before: Everything is energy. You've seen it proven on a physical level using atoms and molecules. Looking at energy from the spiritual perspective, it is what you feel. Have you ever met someone and instantly liked or disliked them? You're feeling their energy. Have you ever walked into a room and it felt creepy? Another room might feel warm and inviting. You are an expert at feeling energy. This is the first communication you ever had as a baby, and you even felt energy in utero. We have been interpreting energy for so long that it is second nature—we don't even notice it. What if you did start to notice the energy around you and how it makes you feel? This awareness is the first step to connecting with your spiritual side.

We learn to work hard when we want something: study, research, step up our efforts, nose to the grindstone, shoulder to the wheel, and PUSH! That is how I was brought up. However, the secret to connecting with your inner self is exactly the opposite: relax, quiet your mind, and see what comes in. Often, what comes in are grocery lists, and that's okay sometimes—we all have those days. These are the days that you come away with a great idea, the answer to a problem you have been wrestling with, or just the feeling of being loved and adored that will keep you on track with your meditation practice.

The goal is to start a meditation practice… this means a little every day, say for fifteen or thirty minutes. If you find it challenging to quiet your mind, you are an over thinker and need to release some of the stress that you're putting on yourself. When I tell clients this, they say, "Oh no, no, no, you don't understand everything I have to do."

I respond, "You don't understand how much calmer and happier you will be when you release your grip on 80 percent of these things. You still do them; just don't overthink them."

When you find your mind spinning about details—I call this hamster brain—adopt your new favorite three little words: *It doesn't matter*. These three little words relieve the stress about things that aren't that important, freeing you up to focus on the things that are.

To get started on a meditation practice, you may enjoy guided meditations. Following a voice and imagery gives your mind something to focus on as you relax your body. You can find guided meditations where you get your music. *Stand in the Light* has them available for download at ComeStandInTheLight.com/CrystalShop/Meditations. You can find all sorts of guided meditations: to balance your chakras, Send Love to Gaia, Let it Go, past life regressions— anything your heart desires.

To help raise my vibrations when I started on my journey, I would do one or two past life regression meditations, and then

I would write them down in a notebook. It's fascinating to go back and look through these experiences. You can also keep a notebook of your dreams if you remember them. Write these down as soon as you wake up or finish your meditation while the details are fresh in your mind.

Once you have mastered the guided meditation, you can try some meditation music. Use what works for distracting and relaxing your mind. Another approach is to focus on the sound of a fan or air conditioner; this will release resistant thoughts and allow your vibration to soar.

People make up all sorts of rules about when and how you "should" meditate and do other spiritual things. What I like most about spirituality is that there aren't many rules and only a few universal laws. The rule I follow is: *Do what works best for you.* People say, "It is best to meditate in the morning," and then they will give you a dissertation on why. I prefer to meditate after lunch. You do what suits your schedule and energy best. You don't have to justify it to anyone, not even to yourself.

Some think meditating means folding yourself into a pretzel, sitting straight up, and chanting. If that works for you, great— do it. I prefer to lie on my massage bed. It helps me relax, and there's a sound I can focus on when my mind wanders. Find a spot in the house, garden, or park you enjoy and where you feel safe. You may have a favorite tree you like to lean against. There may be a little nook under the stairs to set up an altar with a comfortable chair. Try not to use your bed; only use your bed to sleep and make love. You don't need extraneous chaotic energies running around when you want to do either of these; they are too important.

Raising Your Vibration

We each have unique body chemistry, fingerprints, and our own energy signature. When I say vibration, imagine the diagram of a sound wave. If you compare the sound wave of the middle C note on the piano with high C note, you will see a difference in the wave signatures because high C has more waves closer together. We want to use this as a general understanding to avoid getting caught up in our unique signature.

Most people vibrate, for our example, around middle C. People with spiritual gifts vibrate at a high pitch, so go up the scale a ways. Higher-vibrational people are known as empaths because when their vibration goes so high, they can pick up feelings, emotions, and energy from other people—sometimes without trying or wanting to. Go up the scale a little more, and you will find your psychics, mediums, and the like. Another way to look at this is to visualize that if "normal" vibration is at sea level, an empath's vibration would be up in the clouds, and psychics and readers are bouncing off airplanes starting at 18,000 feet.

At this vibrational level, you might be able to communicate with animals, rocks, and plants. I run a crystal shop, and I can hear the crystals loud and clear. When a customer orders a crystal, I use this gift of feeling their vibration to match it with their perfect crystal—not just the type of crystal but the best match of the individual crystal. On a buying trip, I often hear a crystal say, "Put me down cind walk away, lady." When I buy a crystal to resell, it may say, "I'm for you," and not allow me to price and sell it. It usually tells me its name and how it wants to work with me.

Knowing this is possible, people get excited and want their vibration to shoot up to the level they can communicate with angels, guides, and other assorted beings. They expect to achieve this vibrational altitude, and nothing else will change. No, no, mon chérie, things that you are unprepared for will change.

As my own vibration began to rise, I became much more sensitive to sound and light, which became overwhelming very quickly. Commercials on television became disruptive because the energy was changing too fast. The worst thing was that I became allergic and developed a sensitivity to most foods. I had to totally relearn how to eat so as not to trigger an anaphylactic attack. I no longer go out to eat, and fast food is totally off the table (so to speak). It's a good thing I'm a good cook!

Several of my colleagues have similar food issues but not to the extent as mine. This is something you might consider when you look at how high to raise your vibration. Because we professional metaphysicians operate at such a high frequency, the human body is not designed to withstand this frequency. I believe the weakest organ in the body is affected first. My first spiritual teacher, Topaz, had issues with her liver and gallbladder, and another spiritual leader developed cancer in their stomach. So beware of what you ask for; you might get it.

A young lady named Mary called me and said she was receiving all sorts of spiritual messages and didn't know what to do with them. Should she be frightened? Who was sending these messages to her, and were they telling her to do something? Did these come from light or dark entities? Poor Mary was so confused, frightened, and just beside herself. These messages would come day or night. She couldn't find any relief, so she called her friend, a client of mine, who suggested Mary call me.

Mary explained that she had recently attended a yoga retreat where she had three yoga classes per day for nine days. It was during this retreat that the messages began. I tuned into Mary and determined that she didn't have any negative entity attachments; her vibration rose so fast that it opened her up to everything happening around her. Imagine you have a TV antenna on top of your house, and suddenly it's extended sixty feet in the air. You would pick up all sorts of signals you didn't get when the antenna was simply perched on top of your roof; each channel broadcasts fifty or a hundred signals simultaneously. Imagine how confusing it would be to receive all these signals at once.

It was irresponsible of the yoga retreat organizers not to deal with their client's vibration rising so quickly. It's like teaching a group to fly but not teaching them how to land the airplane.

Mary wasn't the only one experiencing this, but she was the only one Spirit brought to me.

Mary and I worked together to give her the education to ground herself when she felt overwhelmed. She learned to distinguish benevolent (good) energy from malevolent (bad) energy. Mary came up with her own answers to help her through. In her case, she found a favorite tree she could sit next to, and the tree helped her to sort out these feelings. Once Mary accepted that she would be receiving messages for the rest of her life, she became comfortable with the process of sifting and sorting to ensure she was safe and protected. She knew I was only a phone call away in case things became too much for her. Today Mary is a very good psychic, although she didn't quit her day job. Instead, she has chosen to use her gifts for her own spiritual development—an excellent choice to be respected and honored.

Another problem with raising your vibration too quickly is that it can make you sick. When I was learning entity clearing and had a rough session, it would put me in bed with no energy; everything else was working fine. This could last several days or weeks. You know how you feel when you overdo it physically? This is worse. I tell my clients before they go through a big powerful clearing to take the next couple of days to rest and recover. We may not be able to see how powerful moving energy is, but we can sure feel it.

Like any other growth, raising your vibration is not linear; it can shoot up, plateau, and sometimes feel like a roller coaster. When does this happen? When Spirit feels you are ready. It doesn't matter when you think you are ready; your guides, angels, and highest self—let's call them Spirit—are in control.

What I have learned the hard way is that if Spirit is trying to teach you something or lead you in a direction and you refuse to listen and go, if you keep charging in the wrong direction, you will get slapped down. You will feel like everything is going wrong and not understand why because nothing has changed. If Spirit wants you to keep still and integrate the information you have received, they will make you sick, so you must stay in bed and be quiet. Say there is something you are supposed to be doing that requires your mental faculties. In that case, Spirit will injure you, so you must stay put and address whatever subject you have been running from. Many people call me, saying some evil entity is trying to hurt them; sometimes, it is their angels for their own good. We must quiet our minds and listen for the whisper.

My Experience of Raising My Vibration

When Spirit decides it is your time to grow, they will lead you to your teacher or healer. They did this for me in October 2018. Unfortunately, they also turned off the flow of clients and income until the end of this growth period in January 2019. During this period, Spirit led me to many unusual and unique experiences.

I had planned a trip to Hot Springs, Arkansas, in January with my husband; I wanted to dig crystals at the independently owned mines. You pay a fee, and what you find, you keep. I rented a short-term apartment on the river with a master suite and a second bedroom with twin beds. As the trip grew closer, my husband decided he didn't want to go to Hot Springs after all. Since there were two extra beds, I asked my two best friends, and they both declined, so I went by myself. Spirit evidently wanted me to have a quiet trip.

When I arrived, I discovered that Hot Springs vendors take the first two weeks of January off, so not much was open. There was also a government shutdown at the time, and most of the tourist attractions were run by the federal government, so they were all shut down. I thought, *Oh well, I'll see what I can find to do on the river.* As many other rivers do, it was drained to a minimum to kill off weeds and unwanted water hazards. So essentially, I was on vacation alone, and nothing was operating, not even the namesake spas, so I couldn't even do a hot springs bath. Spirit must have really wanted me to stay quiet. It wasn't the most exciting vacation, but it was what I needed.

When I got back to work, I found a whole new toolbox designed to make my work much easier during spirit clearings. My vibration had shot way up, and I was receiving messages more clearly than I ever had before. This was a game-changer! This opportunity has allowed me to serve many people much more efficiently, making the work easier for me.

Building Your Spiritual Muscle

If you decide you would like to raise your vibration to make it easier to communicate with your spiritual team, be aware of the trade-offs. Your experience will be different from mine. Yours is unique to you. If something knocks you back a notch or two, instead of getting frustrated, wanting to give up, or feeling attacked, consider what the benefit of this setback might be. Have you missed any signs and symbols that your team has been sending you? There is always a reason for everything that happens, but we aren't always able to figure out what that reason is. If you apply yourself objectively, sometimes you can figure it out or ask your spiritual team, and you may receive the answer. If you can't figure it out, that's okay. Be conscious of what's happening around you and what direction you are being led. The "Why?" isn't usually important; it is "Where do I go from here?" that matters.

I have clients who want ALL the answers. "When did the attachments get on me? Why did they select me? Where was I when it happened? What do they want from me? How would they accomplish their goal? Who are they?" These curious folks are not happy with the answer, "It doesn't matter." If you were diagnosed with the flu, you wouldn't ask your doctor these questions; the doctor wouldn't know who gave you the germ or where you were when you picked it up. Occasionally I find a prominent source for entity attachments, but usually, I can offer a solution, not an explanation.

Regardless of what you plan to do with your higher vibration, learning to energetically protect yourself is an essential first step. As your vibration increases, you get more attention from both sides—the light and the dark. The light welcomes, encourages, and cheers you on now that you may be able to hear them—if only just a little. The dark entities may see you as a threat and try to knock you off your game; that may be why I kept getting sick when I was up and coming.

I call this practice Building Your Spiritual Muscle. When you exercise your body, you begin with a light weight and gradually build up to be able to handle more resistance over time. That is what we are doing here; only it's our spiritual muscle instead of our physical muscles. There are several ways to build this muscle through prayer and training the power of your mind to harmonize with your new vibration.

On the next page is my daily protection prayer; you may edit it to fit your needs. Visualize each section as you read it, either out loud or to yourself. Use it for yourself, your home, your family, or anyone you believe to be clear and will benefit. Start with twice a day, and when you feel yourself growing stronger, you can go down to once a day. Here is how to apply this prayer.

<u>I call upon the Holy Spirit to surround me with the white light of love and divine protection.</u> Visualize a bubble or eggshell surrounding you from your feet to an arm's length above your head.

Fill my bubble with the fluffy sweet white cream of love, pushing out all darkness, with only room for the light. Visualize a giant can of whipped cream above the bubble, filling it up with the sweet white cream of love, and any darkness floats on the top of the cream and spills out.

Fill my bubble with the white light of the Christ consciousness. This one gives me chills!

This bubble will protect me until this prayer is reinforced from all entities and energies that are not my own, reflecting back only love. Visualize a solid mirror on the outside of your bubble. Only love can pass through; everything else bounces off. Use as many layers of silver bubbles as you like.

Daily Protection Prayer

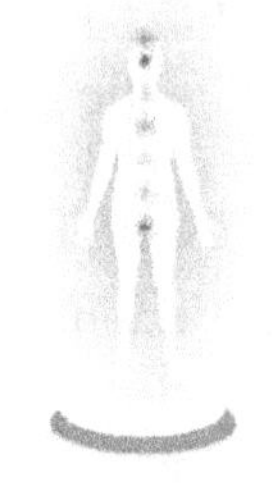

I call upon the Holy Spirit to surround me with the white light of love and divine protection.

Fill my bubble with the fluffy sweet white cream of love, pushing out all darkness, only room for the light.

Fill my bubble with the white light of the Christ consciousness.

This bubble will protect me, until this prayer is reinforced, from all entities and energies that are not my own, reflecting back only love.

Help me walk through this day with grace and ease. As we are, so shall it be, for the highest good of all, with harm to no one.

Amen

Chapter 6
What Are Your Gifts?

I was sitting behind a lady at a presentation on psychic abilities. She raised her hand and said that she didn't have any psychic powers and couldn't see the things she thought she should be able to. As the presenter explained all the different types of *clairs*—a word meaning *clear* in French—it became apparent that this woman expected to have an entire movie-scene experience complete with a soundtrack, special effects, and full viewing ability.

From the 3D perspective that we live in, most of us do not have a movie-scene experience. Instead, we get symbols and clues, unexplained feelings, and signs. We must work with these puzzle pieces like detectives. For example, I met Steve at a metaphysical fair, who came to my table and reported he didn't know why he came to the venue or to the fair and then to me. He asked for a reading, and the information revealed what Steve's guides and angels had been trying to tell him to get his life in order to be able to move forward. Steve's guides and angels led him to this opportunity, and he was wise not to question this guidance but to follow it.

As humans, we think of ourselves as very intelligent and are proud of our ability to reason. Unfortunately, this often works against us in spiritual work. As we receive guidance from Spirit, we can analyze the information and determine whether it makes sense. We can reason our way out of valuable opportunities and into dangerous situations or down less favorable paths. Remember a time when your little voice told you something, but you applied logic and disregarded the guidance? I bet you were sorry when everything was said and done, and you realized you messed up.

An example of someone not listening to their spirit team is a bitter pill. A family in Michigan was celebrating Christmas. The grandparents were visiting from out of town for the occasion and enjoying their four grandchildren and the family pets. Christmas Eve was so much fun—playing games and singing songs. The house was warm and cozy, and there was a roaring fire in the fireplace. The children became upset that Santa would not visit their house as he couldn't come down the chimney because of the fire; he would burn his boots. The parents appeased the kids' concerns by placing the fire embers into a paper bag and putting it in the hallway.

The festivities continued for a few more hours. Eventually, the kids were sent to bed, and the house shut down for the night. As the mother was about to turn out the lights, she heard in her head, "Take the bag of ashes outside and put it in the snow." The mother thought about this and said, "Where did this come from? These ashes have been sitting there for hours, and nothing's happened."

She again heard in her head, "Take the bag of ashes outside and put it in the snow."

She thought *I'm tired. It's cold. It will be fine.* So she turned out the lights and went to bed. During the night, the bag of ashes ignited, burned down the house, and killed all the children, the grandparents, and the pets. Only the mother and father were left. This woman could have saved the lives of her entire family had she only listened to her little voice.

On the other hand, the little voice can rescue you. When I was new to Austin, before the age of smartphones, we had one of the typical Texas deluges, and the city was flooding. I needed to get from north Austin to south Austin and wondered about the best route. I knew the highway would be a nightmare, so I should go through town. I considered which of the two major streets would be best. Then I heard my little voice say, "You want to stop at the store on Guadalupe for face cream. Go that way." I listened to this guidance. I stopped and got my face cream, and got home safely. I turned on the news to find a report saying that the other major street I was considering was flooding, and the video showed cars floating around the street, bumping into each other, and threatening buildings. I was so glad I listened to the guidance of my little voice!

I bet you can think of occasions when you did listen to your little voice, and everything turned out well, and other occasions when you didn't listen and things didn't happen as you wanted. This happens to everyone, but being aware and paying attention to the energy around you allows you to listen to your angels and use this input to your advantage.

Everyone has the ability to intuit energy; let's determine what your strengths are.

There are six *clairs*; you're so good at yours that you don't even notice when you use them. These gifts are activated when tuning in to the vibration of a person, place, or thing or receiving strong energy. You probably have one or two dominant skills and a less powerful one. The more your vibration rises, the more *clairs* come into play. Don't expect you will ever have all of them; that is too much stimulation and overwhelming.

1. Clairvoyance: Clear seeing—either in the mind's eye or in the immediate area.
2. Clairaudience: Clear hearing—the ability to recognize audible information.
3. Clairsentience: Clear feeling—sensing emotions and energies.
4. Clairgustance: Clear tasting—the ability to gain psychic information through taste.
5. Clairalience/Clairolfactance: Clear smelling—detecting an aroma that has no source.
6. Claircognizance: Clear knowing—intrinsic knowledge gained through attunement. Knowing something without knowing how or why you know it.

Clairvoyance is often used to mean all intuition (aka ESP), but it actually refers to vision. When receiving visions, you usually see them within your mind's eye, not walking around the room next to you. You may get a fleeting glimpse, a still image, or a short scene of something playing out. For example, my friend Kaya was visiting, and we were sitting in front of my crystal fireplace, as pictured on TheCrystalWall.com. She turned to me and asked, "Is that a real fireplace? Does the chimney go all the way to the roof?"

I confirmed that it did, and she said, "Good, someone just came down the chimney and walked across the room." Kaya can see outside of her mind's eye.

Many people can see outside of their mind's eye. These people have a unique perspective on life and might be considered a little weird (but who am I calling weird!). They are afraid to tell others what they see, so they keep it to themselves. Sometimes it can be scary, especially if they see something or someone without knowing who or what they are seeing. All of a sudden, someone appears, and then they are gone. Clients tell me stories of their toddler seeing their deceased grandparent sitting in a chair. The child describes the person in such detail that the parent can confirm the identity of the person the child sees.

A psychic reader approached me at a fair and said, "I wish I could see; I've been working on seeing, but so far, no luck."

I said, "That's good; if you are meant to see, you will, in divine time. I don't see because I work with really scary entities; Spirit thought if I could see, I would get scared and stop doing spirit clearings which is what they want me to do."

Being clairvoyant involves a lot of responsibility and is very overwhelming. However, it is nothing to be embarrassed about. If you are clairvoyant and would like help to sort out your visions, seek a metaphysical coach. You will feel better having someone to confide in and be able to confirm your visions. In addition, the coach can often put things into context to help you understand what is being sent to you.

Clairaudience, like clairvoyance, usually occurs in your mind's ear, although not always. In our story about the Christmas fire, the mother was experiencing clairaudience when she heard the warning about putting the bag of ashes outside in the snow. She probably heard it in her mind's ear and disregarded it as a fleeting thought of her own. These messages are usually in the voice that sounds like your thoughts, not some booming voice of God as many expect.

You hear messages from your guides and angels all the time, and you think they're your own thoughts. Sometimes these messages are brilliant ideas that move you forward in your project or your day, and you think of yourself as clever and smart. I'm learning when the idea might have come from me, and when it's too amazing, I know it's from Spirit. My angels remind me when I forget to take something with me. They will redirect my path if they detect a road hazard and generally keep me on a happy and safe path. Learn to hear your spiritual team to make your life easier and more enjoyable.

My team talks to me from behind my right ear as I do readings and channelings for clients. Sometimes they are calm and dignified; other times, they get excited and shout, "Tell them this!" Sometimes I have to write down the way Spirit phrases something; it's impactful and easy for the client to identify with. Other times you might have trouble telling whether what you are saying is coming from you or Spirit. It doesn't matter as long as the information you relay is relevant and valuable to your client or friend.

Clairsentience is one of the most common gifts; almost everyone has been gifted this ability. Clairsentience is the ability to feel incoming signals around you. Becoming more aware of these feelings will confirm this gift in you. Have you ever been walking along and felt sadness and pain you knew wasn't coming from you? You look around and see a child who has fallen and skinned their knee, and they are crying. You felt it before you saw it. In Chapter 7, there's an example of clairsentience in my story of the angry man on the cell phone; I felt it first.

As you become more aware of the energy you are feeling, pay attention to whether the energy is coming from you or an outside source. When I do Reiki, I often feel a fleeting pain, and it can be relatively strong. I ask my team, "Is this mine?" I usually feel my client releasing something that was stuck and bothering them. Just because I felt it doesn't mean they experienced the pain. Clairsentience can be defined as feeling emotions or physical feelings; for example, when a medical medium scans a person, they may feel disturbances in their body as they tune their energy into the client. Unlike physicians, these practitioners may feel the issue so clearly that it is easy for them to determine the source of the imbalance and help their clients.

Many people have an overabundance of clairsentient abilities; these people are called empaths. These folks pick up energy and emotions from others and have trouble distinguishing whether this feeling is theirs or from outside themselves. This makes them stressed and confused, and they have difficulty interpreting what signals they are receiving. For example, let's say you're an empath, and you pass me in an aisle at the grocery store, and I'm irate; you may not even notice. Finally, you get to the end of the aisle, and you're mad and don't know why. If this has ever happened to you, you are an empath and would benefit from developing special protection skills.

A word of warning; empaths shouldn't wear clear stones such as clear quartz, apophyllite, or Herkimer diamonds. These crystals amplify your feelings, so they are great in good situations but unsuitable for empaths. I can feel when a customer is an empath, and if they want to buy clear quartz jewelry, I ask them whether they are empathic and explain why I am refusing to sell to them. I may lose a customer and make people mad, but I'm not here to hurt anyone. Any other quartz is fine; just not clear. One exception: if you have a diamond that's YOUR diamond in your wedding set or earrings you wear regularly and the stone is saturated with your energy, you should be okay, but again be aware of the energies around you.

Clairgustance is the ability to gain energetic signals through taste. Imagine you're driving down the road and begin tasting the cookies your grandma used to make for you. You start thinking about Grandma and the fun you had sitting together at the kitchen table, dunking homemade wonders in your glass of milk and laughing as they fell apart on the way to your mouth. Where did this memory come from? Grandma is probably sitting next to you in the car. Maybe you're going through a hard time, and she wants you to know she loves and supports you; you are not alone.

Taste and smell are strong emotional triggers; Spirit can invoke specific emotions when using these gifts. Once you receive the sensation, you must put on your detective hat to try to figure out what message someone is trying to send you. When I do clearings of malevolent spirits, they use these gifts against me. I won't describe what I taste and smell, but it rhymes with spit! These gifts weren't present when I began my spiritual journey, but as my vibration rose, they developed more robustly.

Clairalience or Clairolfactance is the ability to smell things that do not have a source. You may smell a fragrance that reminds you of your first love. If you smell roses, it may mean

Mother Mary is with you. I had a vendor charge up to me at a fair one time and say, "I don't know who is in my house, but they were a smoker, and they HAVE to go!" Her house guest was experiencing a challenging time which is why she was invited to stay, and we determined that this person's dad smoked heavily. Apparently, his spirit was there to support his little girl in her hour of need and wasn't going anywhere.

Spirit may lead you somewhere through clairolfactance; follow your nose. They may send you a smell or a sound that you feel you need to investigate; this is what I mean by "lead" you. For example, you may smell a pipe or cigar and know that your grandfather is visiting you. Sometimes everyone in the house can detect this etheric smell, as in the case of our friend's smoker dad; other times, this message is only for you.

Melody lived alone with her cat. She woke up in the middle of the night smelling gasoline in her bedroom. She knew there wasn't any gasoline in her bedroom, so she got up to investigate. After searching inside, Melody and the cat went outside to see what they could find, and the detached garage was fully engulfed in flames that were spreading to the house. Spirit woke this lady up with the strong, pungent odor of gasoline to save her and her little cat too. She might have been trapped in the fire had she not been woken up.

Claircognizance is clear knowing—having knowledge of something without knowing how or why you know it. This one is my most potent gift; many people have this one. These folks will make a statement they know to be accurate and follow it with "I don't know why." Eventually, you will drop this phrase and stand empowered with your knowing statement.

My colleague Judy came into my office; she had just had a sonogram of her baby at the OBGYN. "I'm having a girl!"

I looked at her and her baby bump and said, "No, you're not; it's a boy."

Judy said, "Oh no. I've just come from the doctor, and they determined scientifically that it's a girl; we want a girl."

"Sorry," I said, "it's a boy."

She left very frustrated with my insistence that her baby was a boy, contrary to her doctor's diagnosis.

About a week later, she returned to my office and said, "You were right, Cindy. It's a boy."

This trend continued with each colleague who became with child; I could always determine the sex of the baby even if I worked with the father and never saw the mother. I would tune in to the energy of the baby.

Another time I was with my friend Roger who was supposed to meet his friend whom I'd never met. We were driving down the road, and I pointed to a pedestrian and asked, "Is that him?' Sure enough, it was. People get all tangled up in "How did you know…?" That simply isn't important. Never ask a psychic, "How do you know?" I couldn't say how I know the sex of these babies or identify someone on the street that I've never met; I just know because I'm claircognizant.

Now you know the six clairs—ways to intuit energy signals. You have been using these all your life; which ones are the strongest for you?

CHAPTER 7
ENERGIES VS. ENTITIES

We already talked about how everyone feels energy. People describe what they do to protect themselves, such as burning sage and sprinkling holy water, and then they are surprised when I explain that these methods work well for negative *energies* but not for negative *entities*. Imagine the sun beaming through your window. How do you reverse this? Pull down the shade. This represents energy. Now imagine you have a wild mongoose running around your living room. You can pull down the shade, but that won't help with the mongoose situation; you must call the game warden. This represents entities. As The Entity Doctor, I am experienced at getting rid of entities of all types, shapes, and sizes but more about that later.

Energies

People are affected by energies of all types. We have energy coming at us from all around, especially if we are in a crowd or at a high-energy site. A great way to experience a variety of energy is by visiting Sedona, Arizona, where many vortexes exist. When you stay at the resorts outside town, they are calm, peaceful, and relaxing. As I drive into the city, the energy gets intense and shrill; imagine the sound of a mosquito buzzing around your ear zzzzzZZZZZZ. As I drive out of town, the energy seems to deflate, decrescendo, or reduce ZZZzzzzzzz.

Driving away from Sedona, heading home first, we go through conifer forests which give off negative ions that have a calming, soothing effect on us. Eventually, we come to the Meteor Crater Natural Landmark, a park featuring a meteorite impact crater. I have trouble with the energy of meteors; I find it very hot and intense. Imagine the day the meteorite hit the Earth; that is what it feels like to me. I'm always traveling with someone who wants to go see it, so I make a beeline for the gift shop and hide out there until my companion is finished. I have found some excellent deals in that gift shop. I can feel the high pitch energy driving into the park zzzzzZZZZZZ—that mosquito thing again—and feel it release as we drive out again ZZZzzzzzzz.

A bit further down the road, we will find the Petrified Forest National Park, where the energy is ancient and bigger than life. This area is very well grounded, and I feel very calm and loving in this energy. The petrified wood found on this site is millions of years old; the wood from the original tree has been replaced with minerals, usually different forms of quartz. It's fascinating that the crystal takes on the original patterns and colors of the wood it has replaced. Because this energy is so soothing and comforting, I want to stay all day. I make sure to leave with some souvenirs to take the warm, loving energy home with me.

A lot of the energy that people react to comes in from the cosmos. You may have your favorite astrologer that says, "Jupiter is conjunct with Chiron," and other things I don't understand. Eventually, they get down to what this means to you and me. Because I am open to noticing energy, I see when everyone around me seems angry. I had driven down the road watching a car and a truck bounce off each other with anger. They blame each other, but it is the energy affecting them. I've noticed other times when everyone seems tired or out of it. They can't seem to find a thought and hold it. You may have heard the phrase, "That didn't go well; Mercury must be in retrograde." Again, this is energy coming in from the Universe. Because it is so natural to be affected by this energy, you don't notice it unless you pay attention.

We also pick up energy from our beloved Mother Earth; we will call her Gaia. Our bodies always do processes we are unaware of, such as digesting our food and oxygenating our blood, and at the same time, our glands create needed fluids and compounds. Gaia is doing the same but on a much grander scale.

You can feel the different energies that Gaia is emitting and how differently each of these are affecting you. Take your time visualizing and feeling each scenario.

Vision: Imagine the feeling of being in the conifer forest; take in all the calming ions, sweet smells, and silence; take in this energy.

New vision: Imagine standing at the edge of an ocean with your feet sinking into the wet sand, feeling the energy of the gentle whoosh-whoosh-whoosh of the waves, smelling the salt air, and hearing the seagulls cry; take in this energy.

New vision: Imagine standing at the edge of a seething volcano, feeling the heat rise out of the vent, and smelling the sulfur as it burns your nose and stings your lungs. Hear the low roar and the energy build as the magma stirs in preparation for being expelled high into the air; take in this energy.

New vision: Imagine standing in a vast desert; the hot sun bakes down on you as a gentle breeze blows around the sand stinging your legs and making your mouth feel grainy. The only sound is the breeze, and the only smell is hot; take in this energy.

Think back to the variety of Gaia energy you have experienced on a rural hike, in a city, on a mountain, or in a country field. As you pay attention to the vibration around you, you will become more aware of how these different energies make you feel and how you react to each of them.

My amazing trip to Mount Shasta, California, was the most diversified energy I have felt in one place. Every park and section had a very distinctive energy, and earth angels resided there. You can read about this extraordinary experience in my four-part blog at ComeStandInTheLight.com.

Organics also give off energy, although they can also be considered entities: people, animals, and plants. Think back to a time when you felt someone before you saw them; it may be a person or an animal. For example, I remember driving back from lunch one day when an unsettling and chaotic feeling came over me for no apparent reason. I rounded the corner to find a man standing outside the municipal court building on a cell phone. He was clearly agitated, speaking loudly, and gesturing wildly. I realized I felt him before I saw him—he was putting off an incredible amount of angry energy. His aura was giant and red because he was so mad.

Energy that needs to be cleansed from people and places can be left over from arguments or fights, sadness, hopelessness, anger, or desperation. However, if these energies persist long enough, they can permeate Gaia and leave these negative impressions. Blankets are a perfect example of this type of energy. A blanket forms when an area is used in a negative way, as in a POW camp, for example. The prisoners feel disconnected from their quest. They can no longer contribute to the cause. They are separated from their loved ones, and hopelessness and depression set in. This energy becomes engrained on the property and is very difficult to detect and remove.

Places that have seen a lot of war and fighting are very difficult to live peacefully in; the Middle East is a perfect example. There is so much violent energy there that people have a lot of problems getting along with each other.

Energy that has permeated into Gaia may be from the coming of man in the past five to ten thousand years, or it may have been established even before that. It is said that we are currently in our fifth coming of man; imagine all the activity that might have taken place on your property during all this activity going back eons. You may use prayer, sage, holy water, or any other method you like to clear energy.

Entities

Entities are beings—clear and simple. They may be organics, as described above, which means they are currently alive and in the physical world. Entities may be benevolent or friendly beings such as angels, ascended masters, deceased loved ones, aliens (the good ones), animal spirits, some elementals, and many other beings that we are not aware of from the nonphysical realm. These beings watch over us, help us when they can, and send us love and peace.

Benevolent beings help us feel loved and supported. They offer assistance when we are confused about which direction to take in our lives. They can arrange circumstances to help you find the people you are supposed to meet, the job you are supposed to hold or any other experience you have agreed to in this lifetime.

Malevolent or evil energies are the ones I work with as The Entity Doctor. These nonphysical beings include underworlds, Karalians, inner earth beings, aliens (the bad ones), some elementals, and many other types we are unaware of. These beings want to siphon our energy to strengthen themselves; they want to observe us so they can manipulate our development and affect the future of Gaia and all that dwell upon her. Therefore, we need an army of Lightworkers to counteract any adverse effects from these beings. Your increased vibration will help strengthen our army of Lightworkers.

Malevolent entities make you feel angry, depressed, hopeless; any negative emotion they can stir up, they will. They are attracted to addiction, and people with these issues are usually loaded with negative entities. The worse the negative entities can make you feel, the better they feel.

There are beings that are neither benevolent nor malevolent; I consider these beings to be benign. They aren't here to help or hurt us; they are just trying to get by. These include lost souls, some elementals, some dragons, and others. As long as these beings aren't doing anything to harm us, we can leave them alone.

Entities thrive off our emotional energy. Benevolent entities such as our guides and angels receive benefit from our good emotions; love, happiness, joy, and laughter. Malevolent energies receive benefit from our negative emotions. Being conscious of how you feel and the energies you feel around you is important, especially if you suspect you might have uninvited entity attachments.

Entities may be attached to you for a short time or for multiple lifetimes. Clients call me to say they have been told they have an entity. I have rarely found only one entity. Like cockroaches, if you see one, then many are hiding out. People who have had the same entity attachments for multiple lifetimes usually attract more as they go through their lives; the entities all work together to affect the host.

Some people pick up entities right away, while others are immune to getting attachments. I have found some people living around underworld portals with infested family members in a negative energy hurricane with entities whirling around them, and they never seem to get any attachments. These are usually very young souls that haven't had many lifetimes and are still connected and protected by the Creator. I also find people who keep getting reinfected when no source is apparent. These are generally high-vibrational people who go astral traveling while asleep and can pick things up wherever they travel. I pick up attachments when I astral travel; I don't know how to prevent this. I'll bring back three bad ones, share one with my husband, and we can fight all morning until I figure out what's going on and get us cleared up.

Some people want absolutely no entities of any kind around them, not even deceased loved ones or angels. That's like asking to have no pollen around you or insects in your yard; this isn't practical. Many people want a magic prayer, pill, or wand to clear the malevolent energies, and they ask me for advice. Unfortunately, the only way to remove these negative entities is to hire an entity doctor, shaman, or other energy master trained in this type of clearing. Many people call their priest or other religious leaders, but they aren't trained in this type of procedure; you're better off with a professional entity doctor. When capturing lions, get a lion tamer.

When some people find out that they have negative entity attachments, they panic and try to outrun them. They're like a cat with a string tied to its tail. They seek refuge at the home of a friend or relative, attempting to leave the entities at home, not realizing that the entities are attached to them. They are along for the ride. What's worse, some of these attachments may decide they prefer to stay in the home where refuge was sought. They will infest it, leaving the well-intentioned friend or relative with a bigger problem.

Because we live in a 3D world, we try to understand energy and entities from this perspective. People reason that they must have come into physical contact to have picked up an entity, like a flu germ. Because we are dealing with energetic beings, not physical ones, our 3D laws don't apply. As you open up to the wonderful world of Spirit, one challenge is to think outside this 3D limitation. It's not easy to embrace a world we haven't experienced and don't understand. Spirit has attempted to introduce me to other creatures, and because my little 3D mind has trouble grasping that something I don't recognize is a being, I get very frustrated because I'm looking for a torso, limbs, and a head. They will dumb it down for me so I can grasp what they are teaching me.

I spoke with a young man whose girlfriend was the daughter of a black witch—someone who uses magic for negative outcomes and can have ties with dark entities. He was determined to rescue his damsel from this wicked witch and was going to run away with her. I warned him that he couldn't outrun or hide from energy.

He said, "That's okay; I'm a good shot."

I said, "But they don't die."

He hadn't considered that.

Depending on how long and deep they are, most energies can be cleared relatively easily with intention, prayer, sage, and the like. Before moving into a new home, office, or even hotel room, it is a good idea to cleanse the energy and check for entities. For clearing entities, seek the help of a professional. If you attempt to remove negative entities and fail, they can focus on you. I remember a story about an apartment complex with two vengeful ghosts. These two would go from apartment to apartment, spooking and torturing all the animals and confusing and scaring the residents. Finally, one brave man decided to step up to clear the two ghosts, but he wasn't powerful enough. The two ghosts decided to take vengeance on him, which saved the rest of the tenants but made his life miserable. DON'T TRY THIS AT HOME, as they say on TV!

CHAPTER 8
LEARNING THE BUSINESS

As I was learning the intricacies of Spirit clearings, some of the terms used here come from my mentors, and many come from Spirit. I've noticed that the names used for entities do not correspond to other teachings or religions. They may be the same being but use a different name. One example is people ask if I can remove a jinn. I ask them to define a jinn, and they cannot. Upon investigation, a jinn is an underworld entity, but of which strength, or does it depend on the jinn?

Let's define some entities here: the two most common types of entities are lost souls and underworlds.

Lost souls are people who have left their bodies and are trying to find their way into the light to rejoin their soul groups, plan their next soul contract, and get back on their journey. Still, for whatever reason, they are stuck here. Like we who are wearing our bodies, lost souls rally against what they perceive as negative. Think of recent events where protests have taken place; now imagine a bunch of ghosts holding the protest. Also, like we who are still here, lost souls cluster together as we do in cities or towns.

From my experience, a "normal" adult who has never been cleared may have 120 lost soul attachments. Many have more, some less, and others have none at all. Imagine this number of people standing in your living room. They don't mean any harm, but it would get noisy with that many people together; they would spill drinks on the carpet and knock things over. It's just too many in one place. Now imagine all those lost souls talking in your ear at the same time—overwhelming, right? This can make you very uncomfortable, even though they mean no harm.

During classes with Topaz, I watched her check each student at the beginning of class and clear the different types of entities that they carried. When checking someone, she would ask Spirit if the person had any evil entity attachments, which she described as ghosts that had not found their way into the light. I started thinking about that: if someone is stuck here or lost, does that make them evil? I thought, *If I see a puppy in an alley, I wouldn't think, EVIL PUPPY, and run away*. I might think it's lost from its home or mother, and I'd want to help. Maybe these lost souls are simply looking for help too.

My first experience with one of the lost souls occurred when I was studying with Topaz. I felt a sizable person riding on my back with their legs wrapped around my ribcage and squeezing so I couldn't take a deep breath. I called Topaz, and she said to come right over after work.

I went home and asked my husband Matt to drive me to her house.

He said, "If you're having trouble breathing, we should go to the hospital!"

I said, "Not only can they not diagnose this issue at the hospital, they have no idea how to fix it. Take me to Topaz."

When we arrived, Topaz took me into her office, and I lay down on her massage table. She made requests of different councils of Spirits, and I felt the legs unwind from around my ribcage, float into the air, and disappear. I was finally able to take a deep breath. If I didn't believe in lost souls before, I sure do now. Most encounters with lost souls are not this dramatic. Still, I think Spirit wanted me to experience what I would be working with from now on.

Underworlds are from the underworld, which we also know as "hell." Like angels, they have never been in the physical; they have never walked the Earth or any other planet. Also, like angels, they gain nourishment from our energy field. Angels receive benefits from our good emotions: our love, laughter, joy, and happiness. Underworlds benefit from our negative feelings: anger, depression, suicidal thoughts, and addiction. As a result, underworlds want you to feel as bad as possible so they can get as much of your negative energy as possible. Suppose you find yourself having a lot of negative emotions for no particular reason. In that case, you probably want to get checked for underworld attachments. Anyone you know with addiction issues will undoubtedly have underworld attachments; they are like a candy store for these negative beings.

The more underworld attachments you have, the more likely you will have many lost souls rallying against their invasion of you. You may think you are relaxing, watching TV, or playing on a device while there is always a war going on around you. Lost souls are not able to remove the underworlds, so they battle. Animals are also not equipped to remove these bad guys.

Still, they try so hard and feel very defeated when they are unsuccessful at protecting you.

People call me and ask for advice or a prayer to remove these beings; they say they think they have one attachment. These are substantial energy beings, and it takes a professional entity doctor to successfully get them off you. You wouldn't try to remove your own appendix, would you? One client asked if she could befriend the underworlds so they would leave her alone. That's like the rabbit being chased by a pack of wolves and stopping to make friends with them—not a good ending for our friendly rabbit.

Underworlds do not scare, attack, or in any way let you know they are there. They want to be stealthy so that they can follow you around with their claws stuck into you so they can feed off your energy. Anyone who hears voices, feels things moving around their bodies or bed, hears sounds coming from behind a wall, has mysterious pains, or sees things moving around the room, I can assure you these are not underworlds. There is another ailment I call Internal Entities, which we will discuss later. Besides the unexplained negative emotions, you will only know you have underworlds if you are checked by an entity doctor.

I had a client who was being tormented by a late girlfriend. Rodney had been dating Angie, a fun-loving lady who liked to have too much fun. One night, they were driving down the road while Angie was intoxicated, and she thought it'd be fun to hang out of the car window pretending she was a dolphin. Rodney was trying to pull her back into the car when he lost control and hit a tree; Angie flew out of the car to her death.

Because Angie and her family were in league with the dark entities, she refused to go into the light, and she attached to Rodney. He called me for help. I told Angie that she couldn't stay on Rodney; she had the choice of going into the light or being sent into the void.

Topaz said she sent underworlds "to the void," but what exactly does that mean? What does it look like?

I send underworld entities to the void from which there is no return. Angie was a trickster, and even though I witnessed two Archangels escort her into the light, she returned to Rodney. I told her she needed to leave, but she refused, so I had no choice but to send her to the void; she didn't resist. Because she was a trickster, I continued to check on Rodney to ensure he remained clear. I would ask Spirit whether Angie was back, and each time I would hear in my mind in a vast deep booming voice, "She's not coming back." This means ever! So don't opt to go with the dark entities.

The First Clearing

My very first professional clearing was for a massage therapist who was treating me. She had been remodeling a home, which was taking much longer than anticipated. She kept running into roadblocks and problems that prevented the work from moving forward. I went to her house and checked it out. As I was asking Spirit questions, I felt something peeking out of an opening in the ceiling at me. Although there was nothing physical, I could feel the frightened gaze landing on me. I ascertained that there were six underworlds there and several lost souls. *What do I do about this? How do I get rid of them?* I wondered.

I decided to clear the lost souls first as they are not resistant to being returned to the light, but I was told, "Absolutely not until the underworlds are gone; we're not going!" The lost souls felt they were protecting my client and would not leave until they knew she and her home were safe from the evil entities. *So how do I clear these underworlds?*

I felt like the underworlds were joining energy fields to pull strength from each other and form a barrier preventing me from affecting them. I decided to encapsulate each one in a separate transparent bubble to try to break this energy force. As I attempted to take the first underworld into the void, I realized that transparent bubbles were useless as the energy went right through, so I encapsulated each underworld in a black bubble. The energy changed immediately; the combined forces were gone, and I worked with the power of each individual being.

I closed my eyes and imagined the first black bubble in front of me. I was standing on hard ground at the edge of a drop-off; the doors to the void were at the base of the fall. I tried to roll the huge bubble along the hard ground, but the bubble was gelatinous, like a big lumpy water balloon, and very hard to move, in addition to being as big as me. I mustered all my focus, concentration, and spiritual muscle, and HEAVED! The black bubble began to roll slowly. I kept my resolve, and with enough effort, the bubble rolled to the edge of the drop-off and into the void. As I felt this first balloon fall into the void, there was a splash; it felt like a log being thrown into a campfire when all the ashes and cinders fly up and burn your nose, and singe your skin. I confirmed with Spirit that the first underworld was gone; I had achieved my goal.

Spirit encouraged me to keep going. One by one, I fought the remainder of the black bubbles over the edge and into the void.

Some were heavier, some were stinkier, and some would growl and swear at me as I wrestled with them, and they all tried to fight back.

Because I was using all the focus, concentration, and spiritual muscle I had available, I wouldn't call this visualization, but as my consciousness went into this field, standing by the bubble, my body was left behind. Some might call this a trance. As I conquered each underworld, I would cough very violently, and my head would shake "No" brutally. This shaking and coughing directly resulted from being in the toxic energy of the evil being that I was opposing, in addition to the eruption from the void.

After all six underworlds were eliminated, I was exhausted. I felt like I had gone ten rounds with the champ; I had nothing left, but now it's time to address the 156 lost souls. I knew how to send lost souls to the light; I had done so on a small scale before but could only move a maximum of ten at a time. Like most people new to spirituality, I was working with Archangel Michael. I asked him to divide these souls into sixteen groups, and one by one, each group was sent into the light by blowing. I would see the group in my mind's eye in a clear bubble and would blow, and blow, and blow the bubble until it disappeared into the tunnel toward the light. All this blowing was exhausting, and I often hyperventilated. Now I really had no energy left. My client said she noticed an uneasy energy in the living room and showed me where it was. I sent Reiki energy to this spot until I felt a shift and then calmness. I drove home feeling proud of my accomplishment but totally drained physically. I had proven to myself that I can do this, with the help of Spirit.

I thought, *If this is what I'm supposed to do, then fine, but this was REALLY HARD! Isn't there a better way?*

"Stick with us," was the response from Spirit.

CHAPTER 9
RISING HIGHER

We spoke about "Your Vibration" in Chapter 5. The more aware you are of your energy and the energy around you, the easier it is to work with it. Like learning a sport, a language, or an instrument, the more you practice, the better you become. It is easier to practice being aware; open your mind and notice. This will start your vibration rising, and as we discussed, meditation helps tremendously; learning to be calm and quiet, and let's add, happy, or at least satisfied.

People are programmed to complain. When you ask someone how they're doing, they'll tell you everything that's gone wrong for them. Very few will brag about their successes or the beauty around them. When you complain, you stir up negative energy that you've already experienced, keeping it fresh and alive and all over your reality. If that's not the energy you'd like to be living in, then you need to stop complaining, you need to let it go, and move on. Don't stir up negative energy and make it fresh and available to you all the time. We want that negative energy to go away.

When I ask someone what they really want, I usually get a list of things they don't want.

There was a young man at a crystal fair; his company had massive crystals and a large display of smaller crystal items. He was complaining that the fair closed at 4:00 p.m. and they had to be moved out by midnight. I asked him what he wanted to happen, and he replied, "I don't want anything to break, and I don't want to get too tired, and I don't want people to fight or argue, and I don't want to be late."

I said, "Like animals, the Universe doesn't understand the word 'Don't,' so what did you just ask for?"

This young man's eyes got big and round, and a look of horror came over his face.

I said, "You want everything to be packed up safely and quickly. You want everyone to get along, and you want to be finished and in bed at a reasonable time, right?"

He nodded vigorously.

As your vibration rises, it is essential to remain as positive as possible. Phrase things in a positive way. Try not to tell the tale of your flat tire or when someone was rude to you. Let those things go. Don't relive the negative energy of your misfortune. This is where practice comes in. Instead of saying,

"I don't have enough money to pay my rent," say, "I want enough money to pay my rent and go out to a nice dinner." Can you feel the difference in the energy? The Universe responds to the energy you emit, not the words you use. This is crucial for you to understand as you move forward.

When I begin working with clients who want to learn to open their vibration to be more in touch with Spirit, they want to leap over all the trials and the learning and "Be there!" This is like going from a two-foot-tall toddler to a six-foot-tall adult overnight; there will be difficulties. You don't know how to operate those long limbs, and your perspective is thrown off. You bump your head on everything, and nothing fits anymore. You also miss valuable lessons that you will need.

As I was working with Mary from Chapter 5, she wanted to fast-track her growth until it started moving faster than she could process; this also happened to her in the yoga workshop. Remember that we are mere mortals with physical, mental, and emotional limitations. Going too fast can adversely affect any of these areas, so taking baby steps and growing naturally at a pace you can handle is essential. You'll get there. Slow and steady and healthy wins the race.

As your vibration rises to a certain level, you get more attention from both sides. The light beings are thrilled that you are making an effort to join them, adding your uniqueness to the pool of Lightworkers. They note your strengths and plan work for you to help the cause. It is beautiful to be welcomed by the light beings; you are surrounded by love and gratitude.

You also get attention from the dark side. They notice that your light is glowing ever brighter, and the more powerful you become, the more of a threat you might be. They want to squelch the pool of Lightworkers and to do so, they take them on one at a time, attempting to frighten them away and have them turn their backs on the light. The brighter your light shines, the more resistance you get from the dark side.

There was a lady, Monica, in Topaz's class who was a talented medium; she received messages from Spirit easily and clearly. The rest of us were in awe of how she was able to receive information. Although we didn't realize it at the time, we could feel her vibration rising leaps and bounds above the group. Topaz said that the job Spirit had assigned her was Gatekeeper, escorting souls into the light when they needed help. Her light shone so brightly that she attracted the darkest of the dark entities to try to knock her down. She was so aggressively attacked that Topaz didn't know how to help her. Topaz and her mentor were at a loss as to how to help Monica; nothing they tried worked. Monica's mother came to get her and checked her into a mental institution until she could calm down. This is an extreme case, but something to be aware of.

As my skills as The Entity Doctor developed, I got attacked regularly but not to the extent that Monica did. I would go to Topaz for help. Topaz recognized a parallel between Monica's and my situations, and to make sure I wasn't meeting the same fate, Topaz took me to her mentor, Linda Drake, the nationally acclaimed intuitive, medium, channel, and author; she works as a channel for the Abraham group. Linda scanned me and determined I wasn't in danger from the attacks; I needed to stay on top of it and learn to clear myself instead of relying on Topaz.

I asked Linda about clearing lost souls; I was still stuck at ten and huffing and puffing my little heart out. Linda said she sometimes uses a bus or a train to escort the lost souls into the light. That's brilliant! A bus could easily hold fifty souls, and a train could be as long as necessary. However, I limited it to 150 souls initially—any more, and the energy was overwhelming.

As I mentioned, when your vibration rises quickly, and the energy of dark forces fights against this light, it can make you sick. At one time, I was in bed for three weeks as I adapted to the new frequency. For four years, I was often under the weather for a few days or a week at a time. The good news is that you eventually grow out of it when your vibration rises high enough.

My spirit clearings remained pretty much the same, struggling with the black gelatinous bubbles, rolling them along the hard ground and wrestling them into the void. The black bubbles were getting more challenging; some would shape shift and change form and structure inside their bubble as I attempted to move them. Sometimes they put out unpleasant sounds and smells and change size and density to make moving them more difficult.

The void had taken on a structure for me; it was a giant pair of steel doors flush with the ground that slid sideways to open and close with a metallic and fatal BOOM. Remember, this is how Spirit shows this to me; you may experience things totally differently. I soon realized that removing the entities was only part of the clearing; removing the energy left behind is essential for a speedy recovery, whether working on a person, place, or thing.

How can I cleanse energy? Through classes, I learned about the violet flame and its cleansing effects. Healers use it to clear themselves between clients; they cleanse their clients' energy during sessions using the violet flame, and a crystal whisperer even used it to clear crystals after they had been handled by students or used in healing ceremonies. Topaz taught us about the white light of the Christ consciousness, which is pure love.

You will want to get to know the energy of each individually before combining them.

Together these energies should be able to neutralize any negative leftovers. Spirit showed me an image of the bright light strip on a scanner or copy machine to use as an example. I was instructed to shine the violet flame up from the bottom and the white light of the Christ consciousness down from the top. They meet on the ground where the black bubbles are touching and where the energy needs to be sanitized. The light curtain will neutralize any negative energy above or below the ground. The light goes over the drop-off to purify the steel doors to the void and the area around them. The more I used this technique, the more effective it got, but the more taxing it was on my eyes as the lights were so bright.

One day Spirit said, "Put on protective goggles."

These helped immensely, and every time before we begin this cleansing procedure, I hear, "Goggles on!"

I soon learned I needed to cleanse the energy after removing four underworlds, or it became too intense.

After proving to Spirit that I was serious about sticking with clearings and doing what it takes, no matter how difficult, they decided to elevate my vibration. This started when Lorna recommended a healer, Rachel. This lady is incredible in what she can see and how she does her healing. She ran barefoot through my auric field and subconscious to shore up some weak and damaged parts. When she was done, I felt totally different. It felt like Rachel did a spring-cleaning on me, and I needed to figure out how to function from this new perspective while healing the holes from the bad parts she removed.

This healing happened at the end of October 2018, and my business immediately fell to zero. Spirit turned it off to allow me time to heal, grow, and get sorted out. This was a tumultuous time; it was difficult to bounce back from some things that had been removed and released. Much of this time, I was sick; some of the time, I was angry. Some of the time, I was depressed, but all the time, I felt I was going through something big. If you haven't heard this saying, take note: "When you're going through hell, keep going!" I finally came out on the other side in January 2019.

When I returned to work, I discovered that my vibration had shot up tenfold. I had trouble getting my head around it at first, like a teenager who was suddenly three inches taller than the night before with a clumsy learning curve.

Spirit had given me many gifts when I was not working. They built me a ramp going into the void, so I no longer had to shove and roll the black bubble along the hard ground. They put a belt on top of the ramp with which to catch the bubble, wind around it and toss the underworld into the void. This made clearing the bad guys much easier, and I could do clearings faster and more efficiently. I could now remove up to eight underworlds before stopping and cleansing the work area. Before, it was only four.

One problem I encountered was when the belt tossed the underworld into the void, the blowback was intense. Earlier, I equated it to throwing a log into a campfire. Most of the time, it was like throwing a big rock into a pit filled with tar; other times, the pit was filled with poo. Spirit heard my displeasure and gave me a screen that they control; it follows the underworld as they enter the void and blocks most of the unpleasant blowback but not the energy. It reverberates through me like a gong as each one is sent away. I need to include the screen when cleaning the work area; it is such a simple solution to an unbearable problem. Spirit is so brilliant!

There are times, especially during lulls in business when I do a clearing, and it is a little easier. I can accomplish a little more with less effort. Spirit regulates these small lifts in my vibration. The reason I have a lull in business is to focus all my energy on what it takes to accomplish this. The funny part is I never understand what's going on until I experience a new perspective; it all happens in the subconscious. I've stopped sweating the lulls. I expect something really good is about to come around the corner, and it usually does.

As your vibration rises, be prepared for your communication with Spirit to open up. You will receive more symbols, clues, and messages, and your requests to your angels will be answered more frequently. You will notice the energy around you more quickly and be able to avoid unpleasant circumstances by listening to the guidance of your guides and angels. The more you allow yourself to relax and receive, the better results you will get.

CHAPTER 10
WHAT DOES IT FEEL LIKE?

We are all able to feel energy: we are so good at it that we hardly notice. As you read this book, you become more aware of energy than ever before; your energy, other people's energy, the energy from Gaia, and the energy from the Universe. You are embarking on being able to work with energy and Spirit together to have the desired outcome. What does this feel like? Because I do a variety of clearings, healings, and readings, I feel various sensations depending on the type of energy I am working with.

Two important points to remember:

1. Always protect yourself before entering someone else's energy. If they have a disturbance, you want to see it but not take it on yourself. Practice using the Daily Protection Prayer.

2. It is okay to look at someone but to do any work on them, you need to have either their permission; the physical person, their guides and angels; or their highest self's permission. You only need one to say "Yes." If you are

refused permission by all these beings, you must walk away.

We inhabit three dimensions: height, width, and depth; this is all we have to work with. There are an endless number of dimensions. When we meditate or witness a spirit clearing, we leave this three-dimensional world and send our conscious mind into other dimensions. My dog always knows when I am not in my body; the lights are on, but the shades are drawn, and nobody's home. I'll be back, but he knows not to bother me.

To better describe these dimensions, think of an overhead projector that enlarges images from a transparent plastic sheet onto a screen. If you want to build an image with this technology, you might have one transparent plastic sheet with a picture of a cabin, and you put another sheet on top with trees growing around the cabin. Another sheet you put on top might have flower gardens around the cabin and the trees. You get the idea. Let's say each of these transparent plastic sheets is a different dimension.

Now imagine you can only see the contents of the sheet where you are drawn; you can't see the whole picture. What if your mind could jump from sheet to sheet to get a better idea of the entire picture? There may be hundreds of sheets making up this picture. This example demonstrates projecting your consciousness into other areas to be able to connect telepathically.

Beings that I believe can move between and see into different dimensions are insects, specifically flies; every time you pick up the flyswatter, it's mysteriously gone. Mosquitos; one was on your arm; suddenly, it's behind you. And elementals; fairies, gnomes, leprechauns, and the like. I'm sure there are others, but who are they?

When I tune into someone's energy field, I release inhabiting my own body and go to witness them, jumping to their sheet. At first, I feel an impression of their overall energy signature. If there are a lot of negative attachments, I can feel they are dirty, and I get a stomachache, headache, or my throat closes. I can usually feel who this person is; I can pick up on their personality, whether they are outgoing or shy, high-strung or calm, happy or dark. When tuning in to some deceased fathers, they have come across as total flirts. The client says, "Yup, that's my dad."

I often communicate with my client using expressions and phrases that are not natural to me. The client will say, "I can't believe you said that!" They will explain how the phrase is relevant between them and the deceased.

This feels like a thought that's being led, not my own thought. Sometimes it feels like someone is whispering or shouting, "Tell them THIS!" or "Explain THAT!"

I say whatever comes into my head to deliver the purest, most accurate message. When you first start doing readings and you receive a message from Spirit, your instinct is to understand the message and deliver it as it makes sense to you. You must override the will to "clean up the message" and deliver it exactly as it comes. The frustrating part of doing this is you may never understand the depth, complexity, or even the meaning of the messages you deliver.

These messages are not for us; they are for our clients. We have done our job as long as our client grasps the meaning. Sometimes the client will need more time to understand the meaning. This happened to me when someone told me something during a reading that didn't resonate. Hours later, a light bulb flickered on over my head, and suddenly, I understood it, and it was so relevant. If your goal is to do readings for people, be satisfied with the delivery of the message and release the need for understanding or confirmation.

For me, clairaudience comes in behind my right ear like someone is sitting behind me. For Topaz, Spirit spoke to her above her right eyebrow to the back of her head. Wherever and however you intuit, the information is precisely right for you.

Now that you have determined your strongest clair, you may receive a variety of information through this method. Trust what you are getting.

When I began studying with Topaz, I was in a seminar for my work where a crowd was shuffling in to hear the next speaker. I detected an energy presence. Now remember, I'm not clairvoyant; I don't see. This energy seemed to be a skinny man dressed in black with a worn crumpled top hat; he felt like someone out of *Oliver Twist*. He was leaning against the wall at the side of the stage, chewing on a long piece of grass.

I asked, "What are you doing here?"

He said, "I'm waiting for the presentation to begin so I can invade the technology and mess up the presentation. I'm energy, after all; technology is my thing."

I said, "Oh, no, you're not!" I sent him to the void quietly as 100 people gathered around me. The presentation went smoothly with no technological malfunctions.

I can feel and know what something looks like, even without seeing it in my mind's eye. You will find that your gifts will compensate for the ones you aren't blessed with at this time. The higher your vibration rises and the more your stronger clairs develop, the weaker ones will too. You become better able to communicate with Spirit all around you.

I often receive headaches over my right eye, where Topaz receives her information. This is a sign, and I must put on my detective hat to figure out what it means. I can feel pain anywhere when I work on someone, especially when doing Reiki. Sometimes it's a shooting pain indicating a release of energy; other times, it's an injury. I will ask Spirit, "Is this *my* pain?"

If I feel "No," I'll work to find the source or meaning for my client to alleviate this pain. Sometimes we just have to let it go. Sometimes if I feel the pain, my client doesn't, so I move on.

When meeting with clients, I will feel things in my body long before the session begins. I can wake up in the morning feeling entities from people I'm scheduled to talk with but haven't met yet. I feel tension in my body; I may not notice it until I have cleared the entity related to this sensation and my muscles begin to unwind. This happens mostly during underworld clearings. As things are removed, my neck will line up, my joints will pop, and I will start to feel better. Pressure around me changes, causing my ears to pop, and burps to release. When the clearing is finished, and I open my eyes, I feel clearer and more grounded. Colors look brighter. I can breathe more easily, and I feel whole. I assume my client is feeling better too.

When you go to a fireworks display, you can feel the energy of the sound waves pass through your body with each explosion. I also feel this intense vibration when working with very dark entities. Have you ever attended a rock concert and stood before a speaker? The vibrations passing through your body can be much more exhausting than if you selected a location away from the speaker.

It's exhausting when I encounter many of these huge vibrations during a clearing. Of course, what I feel isn't sound waves; it's pure energy.

I've already talked about the coughing and shaking of the head and feet I get when I clear negative energy. I have begun yawning—not a sweet little delicate yawn but a giant open jaw, looking-at-the-back-of-the-throat yawn—as big as can be after a particularly nasty underworld passes into the void. At first, I was concerned that I was inhaling negative energy left behind by this evil being. Soon I learned that the negative energy buildup is being released after the entity has left in the lion's roar yawn.

Sometimes I feel like there are noxious fumes surrounding me, and I can't take a breath. If the underworld is large or powerful, I can feel the intensity of energy as Spirit wraps it up and throws it into the void.

Underworlds feel different from each other; one type shakes, trying to break free. It feels like a weighted can (like a spray paint can) shaking. The most immense underworld usually waits until last, like the anchorman in a game of tug of war. Although they are the biggest, they aren't usually the most powerful; those wait until the end too. Underworlds try to wear you out, sending the smaller and weaker first so they can battle you when you're tired.

I can feel whether an entity is letting go or hanging on by the tension around my eyes and forehead. Again, being aware of the energy around and within you pays off. Not only do you need awareness of what your client is going through, but your body will tell you how successful you are. Very subtle areas in your jaw, around your ears, and your eyebrows will prove whether you are or aren't being effective. If the tension persists, try another technique to release the energy. If you don't feel the release within you, the energy remains on your client.

I also feel when a new underworld has jumped aboard when it thought I was finished. Sometimes they attack my client, and sometimes they come after me—the brave, stupid parasite. If I get an attachment, I stumble over my words. I can't remember the prayers I say daily, and have trouble connecting with Spirit. I will finish the current procedure and then remove the attachment from myself so my client receives 100 percent of my skills and abilities.

When doing scans on people and animals, you tune in to them by sending your consciousness to the subject, starting at the head; you feel in your body what's happening in their body as you scan down. If you have this ability, you are a medical medium. This is a precious gift, and you can help many people. It also helps to have a medical background so that as you receive this information, you can interpret it more accurately. Let's say you get to their solar plexus and feel pain. Is it their gallbladder? Liver? Spleen? You can always ask Spirit, but the more knowledge you have of this area, the better for your accuracy and client.

Staying hydrated when working with energy as a practitioner or client is very important. When I do clearings, I drink a lot of water. Not only does a mass amount of energy pass through you, but so does the water, requiring frequent necessary breaks. I try to avoid doing energy work on long trips. However, when I do work, I still require frequent stops, which prolongs the journey, much to the dismay of the driver and my other traveling companions!

Most people feel when they have a disturbance in their energy field, and many can explain their symptoms that line up precisely with their attachment or ailment. People often describe how suddenly everything is going wrong: they've lost their job or business, their relationship has become rocky, they're restless and upset, and they can't find peace. Their goal is to restore peace in their lives.

What clients feel from a clearing depends on how sensitive they are and how bad the infestation is. Some people only feel a subtle calmness; many people say they feel lighter, breathe more easily, and have a sense of being happy. Some clients are über-sensitive and can feel the entities being pulled off and know when they are completely clear. These people can feel if anything is in their home or on a loved one. They might hear footsteps or things moving around. I work especially closely with these folks.

Receiving a healing is a lovely feeling, whether it's a soul cleansing, Reiki, or ThetaHealing. It feels great for both the practitioner and the client. Before I begin a healing session, I can feel the tension in my body, similar to a clearing; I'm detecting the imbalance. As the healing progresses, I feel my body relax. I can take a nice deep breath, and the emotions of serenity and peace take over.

I always conclude a spirit clearing with a healing, the cutting of cords that do not serve the client, and the healing of the cord cuts and any remaining energy that needs to be transmuted. For many people who have been infested by negative entities for many lifetimes, this feeling is nice but very foreign; it takes a while to adjust to being surrounded by love and protection. When I'm done, you feel yummy, like you're floating on a cloud.

CHAPTER 11
THE DARK AND THE DARKER

Most of the dark entities I battle are from the underworld. The more I work with these beings, the more I discover about them. As my vibration rises and I become more powerful, Spirit shows me the next rung on the ladder. When I was ready, I discovered the underworld portal.

The Dark

"My son's room is always cold, and when he stays there, he doesn't sleep well and is always angry. Can you come to take a look?" asked one of the practitioners at a metaphysical fair.

I was just starting out on this journey, and Spirit brought Fran and me together for the help we both needed. Francine Caruso is a well-respected Reiki master, reader, and channeler. She offers Reiki healing sessions and intuitive messaging in the Austin, Texas, area.

I went to Fran's home and evaluated the entire house and property.

"There is some sort of opening coming in from behind this tall dresser; the underworlds are pouring in through here. There are a bunch of them!" I told her, a little distressed.

Over sixty-five underworlds, and I could only clear one at a time; what do I do about this? I explained to Fran how I usually remove underworlds, rolling them across the ground and blowing them into the void. I told her, "The most I have worked with to date is ten, which exhausts me; I'm unsure how to handle sixty-eight."

Fran said, "I'll help you; we can be more powerful together."

The first task was to close and seal the portal, which was letting the bad guys in. We moved the dresser aside, and I began forming a seal using Reiki energy that I visualized as a tar substance emitting from my hands as Fran held sacred space. I went back and forth over where I felt the opening, overlapping layers to ensure a good seal. Then a layer using an up and down motion to reinforce the first layer of Reiki energy. We needed a break once we were sure the portal was completely sealed. People don't realize how taxing energy practices can be; this was a marathon.

Ready to take on the underworlds, Fran and I sat on the bed, and I encapsulated each one of the sixty-eight in separate black bubbles, which took a while. Then we each got hold of the first bubble and wrestled it over the drop and into the void together. After the fall, Fran would comment, "That was a big one!" or "That one was spitting and cussing," or "That one fought back!"

What Fran was expressing is precisely what I felt. Before this experience, I wasn't sure how much of this was what I imagined and how much I really felt. The answer is both! What happens in your imagination is working on other planes, so though it isn't in our physical 3D reality, it's how your energy affects other energy. When you're new to this, you often feel that you're "making it up" and not really connected. This is normal. Know that you are powerful and making a difference where and how you focus your energy.

The Haunted Bus

One example of focusing energy: Lorna called me and said that her son's friend had recently purchased a 1960s short school bus. Tony and his new bride, Sophie, wanted to refurbish the bus and start a business giving winery tours in the Texas hill country. As a young couple, they were on a shoestring budget and planned to do the work themselves. Tony spent the day unbolting the heavy steel seats from the floor and moving each one to the back of the bus so he could work on fixing the floor. Each seat weighed over 100 pounds, and took a strong man to move it. Tony finished moving the last seat and turned in for the night. The next day Tony came out to finish his work and found all the seats returned to their original positions. They weren't bolted but placed back where they came from.

Tony and Sophie were alarmed at what they found; they live way out in the country where nobody would pass by. Their driveway was very long and winding, and the bus was at the back of the property. This happened overnight in the dark. We were sure that no mortal had moved these heavy steel bus seats. Tony called Lorna, and Lorna called me.

I went to the lovely Hill Country, and Sophie showed me the bus. When I boarded, I could feel the underworld entities scurrying about in a panic. The dark entities know who I am, and they don't like me. I did a scan up and down the aisle and found the portal in the back on the left.

I told Sophie, "The kids were on a field trip, and it was a long drive. They decided to have a séance to pass the time. They opened this portal, and it's been here ever since."

Her eyes got very wide, and she looked terrified. She quickly left me to clear the bus and seal the portal.

People often ask me to check their vehicles for negative attachments, but I rarely find any. It could happen, but it isn't common. The haunted bus is one of the only vehicle infestations I have seen. I believe there wasn't enough consistent negative energy released by the vehicle or the people inside to keep the bad guys interested in staying.

Animals are excellent consultants when I'm trying to identify where an underworld portal is located on a property. I was talking to a client's dog and asked him where the portal was in the house. He said, "Under the bench in the dining room."

I repeated what the dog said, and my client on the phone said, "I can't believe you said that!"

"I didn't; your dog did," I replied.

Animals know where the portals are because they can see them; they can see the underworlds coming out of them, and these underworlds will torment your animals night and day. When you leave for work, only your animals are home alone, so they are the only target of the negative entities who try to feed off your pet's negative energies. When you have your home cleared of negative entities, you do it for yourself, your family, and your furry and feathered friends.

Although 99 percent of the portals I find are underworld, I have uncovered lost soul portals. These portals are like a large closet with several catatonic souls sealed inside. My theory about where these come from is that a furious person died, usually from suicide, and they spit pieces of their soul into these closed rooms. The piece of soul is incomplete, so they appear catatonic. I send these beings to the light for the Creator to care for them.

The Darker

Sara said, "I don't know what's wrong with me; I'm so depressed. This isn't me. I'm usually a happy person, but I just can't shake this feeling."

As I tuned in to Sara, my chest felt like it caved in, my throat closed up, and I could hardly breathe. These reactions aren't totally foreign when I tune in to someone, but they're never this severe. I asked Spirit what I had encountered, and they said to call this a Karalian. I learned that Karalians are the next step up from the underworlds. Think of a large conglomerate company. The hourly workers are the lowest on the totem pole and have the largest population; think of underworlds at this level. Above them are the middle managers, who are more focused, directed, and powerful and eat more. I found that the Karalian has the strength and energy of between thirteen and fifteen underworlds. Remember, my underworld limit is eight before the energy becomes overwhelming. In addition to the Karalian, Sara had fourteen underworlds and over 400 lost souls.

I began clearing the Karalian from Sara, which took most of my energy. Between getting it to the void and cleansing the excess energy, it took almost an hour. This thing felt like an

800-pound gorilla. After taking a break, I proceeded to clear the underworlds, and each of them was an enormously heavy, powerful being. I learned from this experience that Karalians surround themselves with the most powerful and influential underworlds, not your everyday run-of-the-mill underworld. I equate it to a high-ranking politician working only with the most powerful business community members. When I was finished, Sara was exhausted, as was I. She took the weekend to recover, and by Monday, she was back to her happy sweet self.

You might ask, "If you cleanse the energy, why would the client need a recovery period?" I explain it this way: Suppose you cook some fragrant food, and the whole house smells like this dish. You and your family eat all the food, and you clean up the kitchen. You all go out for a while, and when you return, you still smell the food even though there is no direct source left for the smell. Think of this smell as the negative energy left by a Karalian, a portal, or many underworlds. I scrub the energy as much as I can but like the cooking smell, some lingers.

One thing you can do for yourself to help recover from a brutal clearing is to take a nice detox salt bath. Himalayan pink salt is best, but Epsom salt will work too. The salt pulls toxins from your body and helps restore your energy. See my free video at:

https://www.comestandinthelight.com/the-entity-doctor-services/spirit-attachment-removal.

There are also two more videos on this page, "During Your Clearing" and "Tune-ups."

Karalians, like underworlds, want to be as stealthy as possible while making you feel as much negative energy as possible. They do not speak to you, move around in your body, make noises outside of you, or in any way let you know of their presence. If you are experiencing these symptoms, these are internal entities: The Voices (see Chapter 14). Because The Voices will scare you and make you physically uncomfortable, you emit negative energy, which can attract beings from the underworld. These conditions are totally unrelated; a clearing will help the external entities but will not affect the internal entities.

I did spirit clearings for years before I was introduced to underworld portals and Karalians. Call an entity doctor if you suspect you have any of these disturbances. Our unique gifts and training can put you back feeling like yourself again.

Speaking of dark, not all people claiming to be entity doctors or shamans are honest. Make sure you get a recommendation from a trusted source. Everyone's energy is different, so check out websites and videos and go with the person you feel a connection with.

CHAPTER 12
OUT OF AND INTO THIS WORLD

When I was studying with Topaz, she talked about galactic entities; you may know these as aliens. The Grays are the most recognizable, linked to Area 51 in New Mexico. Still, I discovered that there are endless other types of galactics around. Think of all the different species on Earth: mammals, birds, insects, ocean creatures, and reptiles. Now multiply that by the number of planets that may contain life in the Universe. That's a lot of possibilities, and we don't understand what most of them are.

Some galactics are trying to help humanity; others want to study us; and many want to harm us. Galactics come in many different forms or no form at all; some are nonphysical and are studying us to see if this is something they want to take on. I had a client who knew she was a galactic; she said she woke up during an abduction when two of her species were operating on her troubled knee. One looked at the other and exasperatedly said, "We're not making this model again." Human design can be pretty tricky.

I have seen galactics that look like insects with shield-shaped heads, two arms, two legs, and a torso. Another type looks like a fish's head on a human-shaped body. I've noticed that when Spirit is trying to show me a creature that resembles an amoeba, I don't grasp that it is a being, so Spirit must dumb it down and show me two arms, two legs, and a torso so I understand that I am looking at a life-form. Spirit will adapt things so you can relate to and understand their meaning; we are limited to three dimensions, so often, we don't have a point of reference.

Galactic attachments are uncommon; they are usually combined with lost souls and underworlds and are generally not found alone. Once, during a clearing, I detected a galactic, and on tuning in to it, I clearly saw a Gray with a large triangular head, enormous black eyes, and a tiny human-shaped body. I looked at it, and it looked back and said, "I'm supposed to be here; I'm observing."

I said, "No, you can't stay." I called in the Council of Galactic Brotherhood to escort it where it needed to go.

After using the Council of Galactic Brotherhood for many clearings, I learned that this council is very loving, gentle, and sweet. Sometimes I need a "kick-tush" and "take-names" council to affect the tougher galactics.

I asked Spirit who could help me, and they suggested the Council of Galactic Enforcement. This council is better suited to the task of evicting the negative or troublesome galactics.

When I first learned about the effects that galactics have on us in Topaz's class, it was said that when you have trouble finding your words, you drop things and knock stuff over with your elbow; you probably have a galactic attachment. It makes you clumsy and ungrounded. The more I encountered them, the more I learned that the effects can be far-reaching and may be unique to each circumstance.

In most instances, the galactic itself does not attach; many of them are physical, and that would be awkward. They set up nodes deep in the earth that send up virtual attachments, like an antenna that invades the host's body and puts up a strange electronic field that emits signals. They transmit information back to the observing species. Still, this electronic field does not work or play well with our natural energy field and can make the host act irrationally. These poor people are easily irritated and angry; imagine a shrill buzz ringing in your ear constantly. It would drive you crazy.

Sometimes I find two or three transmitters attached to a single person. I must follow the transmitter deep into the earth to the node, the source of the energy. I will cut off all the connections and seal the node into an opaque bag, so it isn't able to supply power to any other transmitter attachment. Like pulling the electrical plug, the transmitters fall over, and I can remove them gently, one at a time. This struggle saves the host much abuse and recovery time. There may be twenty or thirty transmitters being fed by a single node; I assume all the other hosts' invasive antennas fall away also.

I want to go into the earth and snuff out all these embedded nodes, but that is an enormous task! My friend suggested allowing Gaia to heal these, but if it could be done, Gaia would have done so. It may take a team or several teams to snuff these nodes out. Maybe a plan for the future. Perhaps you want to be included?

Abductions

I'm sure everyone has heard the term "Alien abduction." What is this, and how does it work?

I have a family I work with regularly: a mother, Doris, an adult daughter, Amber, and Amber's boyfriend, Keith. Doris and Amber regularly have attachments. Keith was the shining star and always came up clear until, one day, I found two galactic attachments. That's really weird. Going from clear as a bell to two galactic attachments and nothing else—seemingly overnight. What happened?

Upon further examination, I found Keith had an implant on the inside of his left forearm. This wasn't there before; he must have been abducted. Keith told me that he had a very strange and vivid dream about six weeks prior where he was paralyzed, watching unknown creatures do things to him. I discovered that these tiny chips are implanted in people that aliens want to keep track of. These people have been selected as subjects to be experimented on by whatever species has nominated them. Chips have been physically detected in people who have memories of being abducted; the chips are tiny but appear in X-rays.

The chips have two functions: they allow the subject to be tracked by alien scientists like a GPS chip so the subject can always be found for further experimentation. And they keep a file of what has been altered on the subject, like a medical file, so the alien scientists know what to observe and what to change for the next experiment.

Many people are selected as subjects at a very early age. Keith showed me that anyone can be chosen at any age. Keith was a full-grown adult in his mid-twenties.

So how do I keep Keith from becoming an alien science experiment?

Spirit told me to block the chip, so I imagined a lead casing around the tiny implant. Because Keith had two transmitter attachments, I went deep into the earth and deactivated the node they were attached to, then removed them. Now, what to do about the chip? Spirit told me to send a laser beam of pinpoint Reiki energy to this chip and keep the power going until the chip was completely burned out and nonfunctional. If regular Reiki is a watering can and powerful Reiki is a garden hose, I was to use a fire hose of constant energy. It took between twenty and thirty minutes of this pinpoint laser energy. I imagined a stream of fire going into the chip until I saw it twist and turn black; it could no longer transmit location or file information. Keith was now safe.

I have found chips on several people in different places on their bodies. They are usually in an extremity—an arm or a leg—and rarely in the torso or head. Upon deactivating a chip, I had a client return complaining of pain in the area of the burned-up chip. I cannot physically remove it; I just render it useless. I am also unable to reverse any alteration made by the galactic, but the experiment stops there.

Galactics walk among us. I bet you know someone who is obviously from somewhere else. I met a lady named Julie at a fair. She was concerned about entities, so I worked with her for a while. She had me work on her adult son, Jon, who was slightly autistic. When I tuned in to him, it was apparent he was an alien ambassador. He was very high-ranking on his home planet and was here on a very important inspection. I wasn't given the details of Jon and his home planet; I may not have understood them anyway, but I was given the energy of his high status.

Julie was a bit intimidated by the thought that she would be attacked by aliens. I told her, "Definitely not! You are the ambassador's mother, regarded as a queen. You are well protected and respected."

This gave Julie much comfort. Julie has since passed away; I wonder about the reception she received as she crossed.

Inner Earth Beings

Something that I encounter very infrequently, so seldom that I don't routinely ask about them, are called Inner Earth Beings. Many species of beings reside in caves in different dimensions within Gaia. I have found humans, dragons, and other beings that Spirit said I wouldn't understand, so we call them "beings."

Occasionally, these beings get mischievous, lost, or somehow find their way to the Earth's surface into our domain. Still in their dimension, we can't see them, but they can attach to someone. All these things want is to get home. They are brutal with the selected host; they may believe the host knows how to get them home or can find a way. The poor host has no idea what is happening, but they are being energetically brutalized.

The first time I discovered these beings, I was working with Lillian, who is very intuitive. She heard noises she described as snapping and swishing coming from behind the bedroom wall. Her husband heard it too. It wasn't confined to her home; when she traveled, they both heard it coming from behind the hotel room wall or when staying with friends. It seemed to be something associated with Lillian.

After much wringing of hands and gnashing of teeth, we finally identified these creatures. There were seven of them; they were small, gray, and moved very fast. They resembled deep-sea creatures with large eyes, big mouths, stingers, and black hair. They especially didn't like light or loud sounds. They did like Lillian because her vibration was high enough that they could at least get her attention, if not communicate with her.

When I tuned in to them, I got the sense that they had become separated from their tribe and got stuck here; they were asking Lillian for help. I didn't know how to get them home, but I sympathized with their plight. Spirit told me to become a bullet and shoot down into the earth, forming a tunnel for the inner earth beings to follow. The beings helped guide me; they seemed to know their way home. After traveling quite far, we broke through the ceiling of the tribe's home—a vast cave, very deep and wide. This sudden ceiling breach startled the tribe, but as the seven entered their home, I felt a burst of emotions: rejoicing, crying, reuniting, relief, and love. "At last, we are home."

Lillian and her husband no longer hear the noises coming from behind the wall where they stay.

I found one dragon at a time in this situation. Dragons have the traits of cats and can be very demanding and obnoxious. They are also enormous. So a giant dragon with "catitude" is never pretty. The best part of these creatures is the burst of emotion when they return home and see their families and tribe.

Love is the universal theme; we know love very well with our families and friends. We must understand and respect that other beings also feel love. The more we do to strengthen the love in and around our planet, the more everyone, especially Gaia, benefits.

CHAPTER 13
DISCOVERING MORE

As I work with a variety of clients, there are occasions when things go differently than expected. Something extra is happening, or there is an energy I can't define or address. This means that Spirit is about to teach you something new.

When this happens, I will ask Spirit, "Do I know what this is?"

I get "No."

I ask, "Do I know how to clear this?"

Sometimes I get a "Yes" and other times a "No."

Like parents, Spirit wants you to figure it out for yourself. I usually feel like I'm three years old, toddling around in front of my big, tall parents, trying to get my head around something. You know Spirit won't let you fail, but they will let you fall on your tush a few times as you try this and that. If your solution is in the right direction but not quite there yet, Spirit will let you work with your hypothesis until you figure it out; it may take some time, but they are patient. Be confident that Spirit won't give you anything you are not ready to learn.

One of the first things I experienced was what I identified as a scar layer. Although not an external entity and not sentient, this issue causes people a lot of trouble. It appeared to me to be severe damage to one of the etheric bodies that had never healed completely and left a nasty scar. It may have happened in this lifetime, but more often than not, the person has been dealing with it for multiple lifetimes. I became proficient in figuring out how long the damage had been present. The longer the damage, the deeper the imprint of the cause, and the more difficult it is to repair.

Take an example: you were born in the early 1200s in England. When you were four years old, your parents died of the plague. The monarch deems that you must work in the coal mines for the rest of your life as slave labor. What might you feel? Abandoned? Neglected? Abused? Betrayed? Maybe all of the above? If these form scar layers on your soul, these are the emotions you bring back with you every lifetime until you can heal this scar.

I had a client, Harvey, who called me because he was having a terrible time with abandonment. His girlfriend had recently left, and he told me that three wives had left him and two daughters had abandoned him; he was all alone. We did a healing for this scar, and Spirit showed me that five lifetimes ago, Harvey was a toddler living with his parents in a small village in Europe.

One night, Roman soldiers came matching into the town, slaughtered all the adults, and left the children to fend for themselves. Harvey tried to join forces with the other children, but they pushed him away, saying he was just a baby and would drain their food and water but wouldn't be able to help them survive. Harvey starved to death. This was the source of the abandonment issue that Harvey had been living with for his past five lives.

If you hear yourself say, "I don't know why this always happens to me," it indicates that you are repeating a pattern stuck in your energetic field, which may indicate a scar layer. Once someone is an adult, it's virtually impossible to reverse the issue that keeps repeating in this life. A soul-cleansing procedure can relieve this from the client for the next life, and if caught in a young client, there's hope that the issue won't develop in this life. Unfortunately, many adults don't see the immediate benefit, so they don't do this inexpensive healing procedure and set themselves up for another lifetime of repeating the pattern.

I sometimes get the backstory of what happened to cause the damage. If Spirit feels that it will benefit your healing, they will give me the backstory, and I will give it to you. If Spirit wants to heal this and move on, they don't give me the backstory. I have had clients upset with me because I didn't make Spirit tell me the backstory, as if anyone could make Spirit do anything.

I have a client, Ben, a middle-aged man who has been angry all his life. Ben had a lovely fiancée and teenage daughter; he lived in an upscale neighborhood. He had plenty of everything he could want or need, yet he was very angry. When I checked Ben, I found that he had over 500 lost souls and 68 underworlds. Holy cow! I had never seen that many on one person; Ben also had a scar layer. I warned him that during his clearing, he may feel me working on him, and he may feel tired and uncomfortable. The clearing took hours to move all the attachments; later, I found out Ben had gone canoeing, hiking, and to dinner during this time. Where did he find the energy? I was exhausted.

The healing comes at the end of the session. I started the healing as usual, and I saw Ben as an 11-year-old girl in ancient China. She had a large family, and her oldest, very favorite brother was considered an adult by the family. He promised to take 11-year-old Ben to town for the very first time and allow her to select her birthday gift. Eleven-year-old Ben was thrilled to go to town and dressed as finely as possible. Off they went for their big adventure. She was confused when they passed the street with the shops and all the pretty things and headed down a dirty and scary alley.

Big brother knocked on a door where a large, old, poorly dressed, smelly man stood. Ben's brother pushed her into the room so hard that she fell down and chipped a tooth. Eleven-year-old Ben looked up to see her brother receive a large sum of money and disappear as the door closed. The big smelly man turned around and attacked the 11-year-old Ben, raping and beating her until she died. We can understand why Ben was so angry; as the young girl, he was betrayed by someone who was supposed to love and protect him. After the healing, Ben was much more relaxed and didn't get angry as quickly.

After several years of healing scar layers, Spirit now has me call it "soul damage," and they showed me an egg-shaped bubble around someone with a scar from a slash, maybe from a sword that had healed poorly. Soul damage is reversed with a soul cleansing. Soul cleansings are so wonderful, even if you don't have soul damage. They refresh the soul, smoothing out all the bumps, bruises, burns, fine lines, and wrinkles left from living all these past lives. It's like a face-lift for your soul and makes you feel fantastic.

CHAPTER 14
INTERNAL ENTITIES

I was proud of myself for doing a particularly thorough job of clearing and cleansing Rhonda from a dubious number of attachments, double and triple checking to ensure everything was removed, cleansed, and balanced, so I called her to let her know.

"You're clear and protected now; I did some extra to make sure everything is good."

"No, it's still here," Rhonda said. "I can hear it now; it's telling me it won't leave no matter what I do!"

This wasn't the first time I had heard this response; tuning in to Rhonda again, and looking high and low, inside and out, right and left, for this external entity tormenting her, but there was nothing there. Perplexed, I wondered how I could help these people when Spirit was saying they were completely clear? Obviously, there was missing something, but Spirit insisted everything was fine.

The way clients describe this disorder is very similar; many people hear voices, and they can tell you the names and personalities of their tormentors. Many feel something moving around inside their bodies or on or under their beds. Many hear noises coming from another part of the room or behind the wall. One symptom that kept arising took me in a bizarre direction, but who's to say what is bizarre in this business?

Many people—both men and women—complain that they feel like they are being raped constantly; it never stops. As you can imagine, they're at their wit's end. They can't take anymore. I sat with Spirit to see if I could put the puzzle pieces together. What came to me was that the dark side has nine layers of beings in the hierarchy. The underworlds are level one, the weakest; the devil is level nine; demons are level eight; and sub-demons are level seven. The upper echelon doesn't attach to people; they want land and territory. Spirit said these beings sexually attacking my clients were incubi and succubi.

Wikipedia defines these terms as follows: an incubus is the male form of this dark entity, and a succubus is the female. We will call them Buses for short. We know we are dealing with energetic beings, and energy doesn't have gender; either being can take the form of either sex as necessary. I determined that an incubus attaches to a person, and a succubus is transient. They make the rounds.

Spirit also explained that I had conquered level one, the underworlds. At the time, I was working up to level two—the Karalians. The Buses are levels four or five. I asked how I could remove them and was told, "You can't."

"So I can't help my client?"

"No."

"I can't give them any relief? Guidance? Comfort?"

"No."

This was a hard blow—Spirit telling me I was helpless to do anything. I had a hard time accepting it; after all, I am the boss, and I rule the world; there must be something?

"No" was all I received from Spirit, knocking me off my pedestal and crashing back to Earth, a mere mortal.

My clients had a hard time accepting that I could not help them; they pleaded and begged and broke my heart.

I continued to talk with clients with similar complaints, and the list grew. Many had objects that moved around; other people heard and felt what my client was experiencing. Some saw an apparition; some have pictures on their phones, and they can prove it. Many feel someone leaning over them as they sleep, and some hear their name being called from another room.

This was getting to be too much to let go of, and I decided to call a meeting of my closest and most connected colleagues, Mitchy and Kaya. I explained the situation to them, and it was suggested that this was a result of the energy felt by 4G and 5G signals. Some clients have felt this way for twenty years so that probably wasn't the culprit. Diet was discussed, as was all the GMOs and Frankenfood that's out there today. Mitchy specializes in treating PTSD. Maybe it was related to that? This meeting generated many theories but no conclusions. I even had Mitchy work with one of these clients who was particularly tenacious, but in the end, Mitchy couldn't help her either.

I was watching a YouTube video about the conscious mind and the veil separating it from the subconscious, and I got an idea.

I sat and talked with Spirit.

"Is this ailment dealing with the subconscious mind? Is this why entity doctors can't feel an external presence on the client?"

Spirit affirmed this as accurate.

"Does this result from the 88 percent of the unreachable mind attacking the 12 percent of the waking mind?"

Spirit affirmed again.

No wonder I couldn't remove it from the outside; what could I do? I'm a spiritual doctor, not an emotional doctor.

One of my colleagues teaches ThetaHealing™, a process of accessing the subconscious mind through a questioning process and asking the Creator of All That Is to reprogram the negative issue, like replacing a corrupt program on your hard drive. Studying ThetaHealing and working with Creator opened a whole new level of vibration for me. It has made tasks easier by using this powerful energy. I used to get stuck where negative energy took a long time to release and clear; now I can ask Creator to help, and things clear right up.

Sandra came to me complaining that she and her family heard footsteps from upstairs when they were downstairs. She would see and feel something flying above her bed. She felt like someone was always watching her. I did a ThetaHealing session with Sandra. We found the bottom belief that wasn't serving her. Creator reprogrammed it, and the noises and feelings went away. Sandra had a mild case of The Voices. Most patients are much more severe. For the very severe cases or the ones that want someone to "fix it" and not do the work themselves, I recommend they see a therapist, counselor, or psychologist. For people who are very badly off, a psychiatrist is in order, as they may need some medication if they are overly disturbed.

You may ask, "If one person is generating a disturbance, how can others see, hear, smell, and feel it?"

Excellent question. Have you ever heard of poltergeists? These are supposed to be child ghosts that enjoy causing mischief. We have no idea how powerful our energy is. We haven't studied it for many generations, and we take it for granted that we stop at the end of our skin. In reality, our energy field goes well beyond our physical bodies and can fill an entire room. We have the capability of moving objects and making noises beyond our physical bodies. Families notice that they only see and hear things when the afflicted individual is present. If that person is not home, all is quiet.

Clients get very angry when I explain that they have internal entities called The Voices. They will argue and keep giving me examples of how uncomfortable they are and how this is an external entity tormenting them. All the symptoms they list confirm The Voices:

"It is inside my head; it knows my thoughts."

"I feel like they are taking over my thoughts and actions."

"I feel like I have lost control of my life over this."

"They are always inside my body and mind."

Some say, "So this is all in my head?"

I say, "Not really; it **is** in your head, but you can't control it."

One client called it an "internal entity." I think that is a perfect description. Since it is an imbalance inside a person's head, I can't reach in from the outside and make it go away or pluck it off like a piece of lint. It's a scary proposition to think someone could reach inside your head and program your thoughts in your conscious and subconscious minds. Leave that to the Creator!

Most people are looking for a magic wand to make this disappear. They don't want to put their time and effort into getting better; they want you to do it for them. They will beg and plead, "Won't you fix this for me?" but will not schedule a ThetaHealing session or do anything to help themselves.

I had one client who did three ThetaHealing sessions and confessed, "I don't think this is ever going to go away."

I said. "If this has been affecting you for nine lifetimes, it will take more than three hours to fix."

Would you really expect to lose fifty pounds in three days of dieting? It's the same thing.

The more tormented these poor folks become, the more negative energy they put out, so the more the underworlds are attracted to them. About half the time I find The Voices, I also find external attachments. I explain to the client that we must remove the attachments before we can begin to work on The Voices. I explain that these are two different issues and doing the spirit clearing won't affect the symptoms they are feeling with The Voices. They say they understand, but they get mad when the spirit clearing doesn't fix The Voices.

The Voices is a complicated ailment because it's emotional, mental, and usually past life based, not purely spiritual. How can you tell the difference? Spiritually-based negative entities include underworlds and Karalians. They are stealthy and don't want to alert you to their presence. They make you depressed, angry, or feel bad about yourself and your life. The Voices want to scare and control you. They let you know they are with you; you hear them and feel them move around. You may think that these are separate from you. Yet it very well may be your subconscious, possibly past life personalities, reawakening. Both issues will require help to fix. Now you can determine what type of professional will best serve you.

Chapter 15
A Sunnier Outlook

Raising your vibration, connecting with Spirit, and becoming a calmer, happier you doesn't involve a lot of time and effort; all it takes is a little rewiring to adjust your perspective. Once you allow your spiritual team to help you find and stay on your path, it's much easier and more pleasant than going it alone. You encounter less resistance, and manifestation is easier to accomplish.

I had a client, Eric, a man in his mid-thirties who wanted the American dream: love, family, and a home. He wanted to buy a house to begin investing the money he paid out in rent. Eric did a coaching package with me, so he had six sessions to get himself sorted out. He would complain that he so wanted a house of his own where nobody could tell him how many animals could live there or what color he could paint his walls.

Eric would lament over how he kept looking, but when he found the right fit, the contract wouldn't go through. Eric spent most of his energy missing the house he didn't have instead of picturing himself in the ideal home.

Eric and I worked on visualizing what his home would look, smell, and feel like. How would he feel when he cut the grass and sat on the front porch watching the neighbors walk their dogs? And when he would smell the barbecue brisket from the friend next door and get the invite to "Come join us for dinner?" Eric's homework was to keep this visualization going and not mourn the lack of a house. This worked! Eric found his ideal house for a fair price in an upscale neighborhood near people his age and demographic. The more Eric saw himself in this home, the smoother the process went. The house passed all the inspections. The owners made all the improvements Eric requested, and the contract process was a breeze.

Soon after, Eric moved into his dream house and went out to buy furniture to make it the home he always wanted. One of the salespeople he was working with was a lovely young lady, Gloria. She was very excited about Eric's new home and bright future. Their energy immediately meshed, and Eric asked Gloria out to dinner. Everything was falling into place for Eric, and he and Gloria became a couple very quickly. She helped him design and move into his home, and within six months, she was living there too. A year later, they were married and are now expecting their first child. They have four dogs and two cats and have painted their home in their favorite bright, happy colors. Eric and Gloria have a beautiful life ahead of them. All this manifested when Eric changed his perspective.

My client Zula is on her path to raise her vibration and grow closer to her guides and angels. She is a beautiful young lady dabbling in acting and other creative outlets. Zula is left-brained, so she has her life all figured out. She and her sister were raised by their single mother, and Zula felt an obligation to make sure her mom was taken care of in her golden years.

She decided the answer was to become a nurse. She said, "I will make a good salary, have job security, and have a reliable occupation that I can do anywhere. It all makes sense."

What I never heard when I asked her "Why a nurse?" was "To help people," "Because I love it," or even "Because the medical field is fascinating."

She said, "Because I'm a healer."

There is a boatload of healers out there that aren't medically trained; I'm one.

Despite Zula's guides, angels, and me trying to wave her off, she willfully stuck to her plan. Zula did all her preparation classes, tested, and was accepted to nursing school. She focused diligently on her studies and earned top scores as one of the leaders in the class. Zula was doing great academically.

Emotionally, she was a mess.

"I hate it! This is no fun. I'm doing well, but I don't like it. I'm so depressed," Zula would tell me.

Now we all hate to hear, "I told you so." Rest assured that your angels will never say this to you. They love you very much and are very nurturing (although mine can get snarky like I am).

Zula intended to finish the semester but decided that she was so unhappy that she just called it quits. I was very proud of her for abandoning this plan that she had in place for so long; that was very brave.

Zula's vibration rose so high that she was visited by a rainbow succession of dragons, one color at a time. Each had a story it wanted Zula to tell. Not only could she write the story to the satisfaction of the dragon, but she could also see and paint the pictures the dragon wanted to be portrayed. This is an excellent example of partnering through channeling, and it helps children understand spiritual lessons. How much better could this have turned out? See her work on Amazon.com under Zula Casablanca. Spirit saw in Zula much greater things than she imagined.

People think that if you're spiritual, everything is easy and pleasant, people are sweet and loving, and there are never disturbances. We are talking about the blueprint for your life path so that you can experience all the lessons on your list. We don't know what these lessons are when we are on this side of the veil; that's why your team must lead you, and you must listen. Lessons are rarely easy or pleasant. Adjusting your perspective to remain calm and grounded during this roller-coaster ride will put out the type of energy you want in return. You have power and control over your little corner of the world.

CHAPTER 16
YOUR TOOLBOX

We've talked a lot about how you can raise your vibration to be able to connect with your spiritual team. Let's gather these tools together and put them in your toolbox so you can access them whenever you like. As you know, Spirit gifts me with energetic tools, both large and small, when I am ready to master them. They will do the same for you. It may require you to put on your detective hat to grasp the new tool, figure out what it is, and how to use it, but Spirit is patient and will use different communication methods to teach you.

The Attitude of Gratitude

Your strongest tool, by far, is the attitude of gratitude; the energy you put out is the energy you get back:

- Being aware and happy for who you are: intelligent, beautiful, interested in better things for yourself.
- For what you have. Look around you. You have all the creature comforts.

- You also have gifts you may have just discovered or known about your whole life. Appreciate them. They make you unique.
- For where you live. Appreciation for the energy of the home you have created for yourself and your family.

It's fine to aspire to move up, but let's appreciate where we are in this moment. How far you have come and how far you will go!

Be proud of yourself! Don't use "Yeah, but…" to tear yourself down. There may be more goals to achieve, but we are celebrating the ones we have already accomplished for now. Replace "Yeah, but…" with "Yay ME!!!"

A little self-love goes a long way, and who better deserves it than YOU? Implementing this tool will significantly tune your vibration and adjust your attitude, making you a happier person overall.

Find Calm

Part of finding things to appreciate is slowing down, taking a step back, and being patient. Release the grip and stop sweating the small stuff. Don't sweat the big stuff either; just get it done; no drama is required. This frees up your energy and emotions, allowing in peace and calm. It also allows you to listen to your spiritual team's guidance, and isn't it nicer to feel this support than trying to do it all by yourself?

Protect Yourself

Be aware of the energy you put out and be mindful of the energy around you. Protect yourself from encountering unwanted energy by using the Daily Protection Prayer from Chapter 5. When you begin, use it twice daily; it only takes thirty seconds or so. Once you feel the continuity of the energy, you can go down to once a day. Maybe you are going into a situation with many people, like a stadium, concert, or grocery store. In that case, you might use it before entering. You will become good at knowing when it will help you.

Set Your Intentions

Telling Spirit what you want is the practice of setting your intention. This is a vital tool to have active in your toolbox. Setting your intention puts the energy into the Universe that you want. It may be a small intention such as:

"Angels, please get me to and from my destination swiftly, safely, and without incident."

I say this when I get into the car.

Always use the words that work best for you. It might be something big, like:

"Angels, please find me the job that is in my best and highest good where I will be happy and earn $150,000 yearly OR BETTER." Never forget the "or better" or "or more." We don't want to limit ourselves. Spirit may have much more planned for you than you could imagine; open up and listen.

Communicate

Several divination tools are available at your discretion to ask your team Yes–No questions. They won't address the Who? What? When? Where? or How? Only the "Yes" and "No."

My favorite tool is a pendulum; it has become an extension of myself, like your cell phone, always in my hand. There's a free video on "How to Use a Pendulum" at ComeStandintheLight.com/CrystalShop/Pendulum. There you can see examples of pendulums.

Other tools available are oracle cards, although these are open to broad interpretation. There is a bobber; it works similarly to a pendulum but is a metal rod on a handle. Some people like stones called "runes," but you must be trained to read them. Use what resonates with you; only you can determine what is right and wrong for you.

There is an art to asking the question regardless of which divination tool you choose. See "How to Use a Pendulum" at ComeStandintheLight.com/CrystalShop/Pendulum for guidance on getting the most accurate answers. If you are surprised by the answer, you have reached Spirit. I sometimes ask, "Am I influencing how this pendulum is moving?" to ensure I'm not imposing my views on the situation. We want to be totally objective to hear what Spirit has to say.

Meditate

In Chapter 5, we talked about implementing a meditation practice and taking a few well-deserved minutes every day to yourself to relax, unwind, and let everything go. This practice will significantly enhance your heightened vibration. Topaz told us that she would take the first five or ten minutes to vent, unwind, make lists, and generally spin. Then she would say, "All this has been done; now we can be still." And then take the next ten or twenty minutes to enjoy her release.

Meditation is the only time investment for the tools we have discussed; everything else is adjusting your perspective.

There are short, powerful meditations that you can sneak in on your lunch break, such as the six-minute "Love Meditation" or the eight-minute "Let it Go." Keep yourself healthy and balanced with the slow, relaxing "Chakra Meditation." It will leave you feeling calm, peaceful, and amazing. Find these at ComeStandintheLight.com/CrystalShop/Meditations.

Community

If you can find some like-minded people to connect with, it will help accelerate your vibrational increase. Hearing their stories and telling them yours is very healing and gives you confirmation that you are indeed growing. In-person is best, but online is excellent as well. Watch https://www.facebook.com/comestandinthelight for groups. Check with local metaphysical shops, local coffee shops, or online for meetings.

You Have What You Need

You have everything you need to move forward with your spiritual practice, raise your vibration, and connect with your guides and angels. If you want support and guidance, I have classes and private sessions available or check your local area.

Each of us is unique in our energy signature. Spirit will help you find the teacher for your best and highest good in your current situation. Be prepared to move on to new teachers as you progress.

You are in control. You can take this as far as you like with Spirit's help. Now soar!

REFERENCES

Linda Drake

https://www.lindadrakeconsulting.com/

Life Path Healer and Spiritual Life Coach, Author

Francine Caruso

The Spirit Connection

Austin, Texas

francine.caruso@yahoo.com

Zula Casablanca

Author, Illustrator, Channeler, Photographer

Amazon.com/Zula Casablanca

CURIOUS TO KNOW MORE?

In addition to spirit clearings and healings, Cindy Hallett offers readings, Reiki energy, and ThetaHealing™ sessions anywhere in the world.

Take classes from Cindy Hallett, The Entity Doctor, about how the other side works.

Learn from America's #1 leading expert in spirit clearing.

**Call 833-612-4100
or visit
ComeStandInTheLight.com**

<u>NOTES</u>